FINDING VOICE

Introductory Lessons to Teach Reading and Writing of Complex Text

by Nancy Dean *with* Natalie Danaher

MAUPIN HOUSE BY
CAPSTONE PROFESSIONAL
a capstone imprint

Finding Voice: Introductory Lessons to Teach Reading and Writing of Complex Text

By Nancy Dean with Natalie Danaher

Cover Design: Cynthia Della-Rovere
Book Design: Cynthia Della-Rovere

Library of Congress Cataloging-in-Publication Data
Cataloging-in-publication information is on file with the Library of Congress.

978-1-4966-0607-5 (pbk.)
978-1-4966-0610-5 (eBook PDF)
978-1-4966-0613-6 (eBook)

Text and Image Credits:
Extract from *Mulan* by Michaela Morgan, ORT Traditional Tales (OUP, 2011), text, copyright © Michaela Morgan 2011, reprinted by permission of Oxford University Press.

Extract from and cover image of *East of the Sun, West of the Moon* by Chris Powling illustrated by Violeta Dabija, ORT Traditional Tales (OUP, 2011), text, copyright © Chris Powling 2011, illustrations copyright © Oxford University Press 2011, reprinted by permission of Oxford University Press.

Capstone Studio: Karon Dubke, Cover; Shutterstock: BrAt82, 166

Capstone Professional publishes professional resources for K-12 educators. Contact us for tailored, in-school training or to schedule an author for a workshop or conference. Visit www.capstonepd.com for free lesson plan downloads.

Maupin House Publishing, Inc. by Capstone Professional
1710 Roe Crest Drive
North Mankato, MN 56003
www.capstonepd.com
888-262-6135
info@capstonepd.com

Dedication

For Lucy, Gabriella, and Violet:
The Three Muses
And
For Molly

Acknowledgments

From Nancy

I could not have completed this project without the thoughtful guidance of Karen Soll and Emily Raij of Capstone Professional. Heartfelt thanks go to both of them for their insight, care, and support.

I continue to appreciate my professional and personal connections to Christy Gabbard, who believes in the power of teaching and is always ready with a word of encouragement and an astute suggestion.

P.K. Yonge Developmental Research School in Gainesville, Florida, is an extraordinary school, filled with skilled and dedicated school leaders and teachers. For this book I owe a special debt to Carrie Geiger, Supervisor of Instructional Practice, for paving my way into the elementary classrooms.

A "thank you" is hardly adequate to Blake Beckett, an amazing third-grade teacher at P.K. Yonge. Blake field-tested many of the lessons, provided samples of student work, and demonstrated again and again that teaching reading and writing is not just rigorous but also joyful and engaging.

A very special thanks is due to the third-grade students in Blake Beckett's class at P.K. Yonge. They showed me that the text and lessons in this book are **not** too hard for elementary students. Their enthusiasm, diligence, and intellectual courage take my breath away each time I visit their classroom.

Thanks always to Tom, voice wizard, who understands and remembers.

From Natalie

A special thanks to Margaret Mary Policastro, Becky McTague, and Diane Mazeski of Roosevelt University. You are all wonderful teachers of teachers.

Thanks to David Wood, Loretta Koulias, and all the teachers, students, and families of Our Lady of the Wayside School.

Thanks to my parents, Anne and Mike, for their generous support and encouragement, and particularly to my love, Michael.

Table of Contents

Introduction to the Power of Voice

Finding Voice is a teacher resource book designed to help upper elementary school students read closely and carefully and write powerfully, expressing their own distinctive personalities. It is a collection of lessons and activities to teach students to understand voice in reading and to use the elements of voice effectively in their own writing. So what exactly is voice?

Voice is what makes reading interesting. It's what makes us say, "I'll bet that book is by J. K. Rowling or Lemony Snicket." Voice gives color and texture to writing. It is the expression of personality. Voice can be strong and distinctive or reserved and generic, but all writing has voice of some kind. The study of voice helps students appreciate the power of language and teaches them to use the effective techniques that experienced authors use.

Voice comes from **conscious choices**. Every good author **intentionally** chooses to produce a certain effect. Good writing is no accident! As you help students examine the conscious choices authors make, encourage them to answer some fundamental questions:

1. What is the author saying? (What does the work mean?)
2. How do you know? (What evidence can you find in the work that reveals the author's meaning?)
3. How does the author do that? (What specific tools does the author choose to construct meaning, and how does he/she use these tools?)

Learning to answer these questions will help students make their own effective choices as young authors. Just as visual artists must master tools such as color, perspective, light, and texture, authors must master the tools they use to create the effect they want: **the elements of voice.** The elements of voice that we explore in this book are

- word choice,
- detail,
- imagery,
- figurative language, and
- tone.

Word choice refers to the selection of words that are clear, concrete, and exact. Word choice is the foundation of all good writing. **Detail** refers to the facts, observations, and incidents that develop a topic. Writing without detail is flat and boring. **Imagery** is the use of words to convey a sensory experience (what you hear, see, smell, taste, or touch). Imagery brings life to writing and makes it seem real. **Figurative language** is the use of words in unusual ways to reveal meaning that is not literal and makes the reader think. Finally, **tone** is the expression of attitude in writing. Writers convey tone through the use of word choice, detail, imagery, and figurative language. *Finding Voice* explores each element of voice separately in the five chapters that follow.

The lessons in *Finding Voice* have a consistent format. Each lesson begins with a passage for students (or you) to read and discuss ("Consider the text"). Then you guide your students through a conversation based on two questions about the passage ("Take a deeper look"). These are not comprehension questions (we assume students will understand the passages; but if they don't, guide and support them through the passage).

The two questions direct students' attention to the aspect of voice considered in the specific lesson. Lastly, students will try creating their own clear voice in writing, using the specific text in the lesson as a model ("Now you try it").

Students may find some of the passages quite challenging. If so, it might be useful to modify the approach. Here are some suggestions:

1. Preview difficult vocabulary before reading the text.
2. Slow down and read the text aloud several times, discussing difficult parts with students.
3. Differentiate for struggling readers. That might mean cutting the passage or focusing on one sentence or phrase that models the purpose of the lesson.

Although it may take some time, it is important for students to tackle passages that are complex. To help students become more comfortable with difficult text, the passages in *Finding Voice* are short, thus not overwhelming, making these lessons a good place to start with the close reading of complex text.

Finding Voice is not a complete curriculum. It is designed to strengthen the regular language arts or reading curriculum. We recommend using the lessons two or three times a week to stimulate interest in the critical reading of complex text, the understanding of how great writers use voice, and the development of personal voice in writing. Of course, students won't master everything at once, but they will learn to think about reading and writing differently as you help them work through the lessons and activities of this book.

You may run off copies of the lessons and activities for classes of students, as specified in the copyright agreement; or you may project the quotations and have students complete the exercises on their own paper. However you decide to use the lessons, it is important to remember that students need each lesson's text in front of them for analysis and as a model for their own writing.

Each lesson will take between 10 and 20 minutes, depending on the lesson's difficulty and student interest. The lessons are complete in themselves, and the order of lessons is flexible. We do recommend, however, that you go through at least one cycle of lessons from the word choice, detail, imagery, and figurative language chapters before you tackle tone. Understanding tone requires a prior knowledge of the other voice elements.

We have included a section called "Commentary and Suggestions for Teachers" with each lesson. These are our suggestions only and by no means exhaust the possible responses to the text, questions, and activities. The intent is to spark discussion and encourage thinking. We fully acknowledge and recognize you, the classroom teacher, as the expert, and we honor your ideas and insights.

We hope that *Finding Voice* is helpful, interesting, and challenging for you and your students. We wish you well as you help shape your students' voices.

Nancy and Natalie

Lessons

Wonderful Words

Introduction

Our lives are filled with words. Words often wake us up in the morning, keep us company at breakfast, travel with us throughout the day, and comfort us as we fall asleep. Words are the bedrock of communication, especially when it comes to reading and writing. Good readers make friends with words. They think about the different meanings a word may have and learn to figure out just what a word means in a particular sentence. Good readers can participate in the world of stories and grow in understanding of how the world works because of words.

For authors, words are foundational. Words are the author's palette. Just as an artist uses color and texture to create an experience for the viewer, an author uses words to build a story, express an opinion, or impart knowledge. Word choice is purposeful and studied, no easy task. In order to write well, an author has to find the perfect word.

The perfect word is **clear**, **concrete**, and **exact**: It says exactly what the author wants it to say, is specific, and creates a particular picture. The perfect word precisely expresses the feeling or idea an author wants to get across. It is not always easy to find the perfect word, however. To find perfect words, young authors need to experiment, to learn new words, to stretch themselves a little. They can ask someone for a better word. They can look for synonyms in a dictionary or on the computer (always checking that the synonym works in this context). Or they can learn to use a thesaurus, one of the author's most valuable tools.

Words cannot be clear, concrete, and exact unless young authors also understand the shades of meaning a word brings with it. Along with their literal definitions, words can suggest feelings, and it's essential to know both aspects of a word's meaning. For example, the words "slender" and "skinny" have roughly the same meaning: having virtually no excess weight. However, the words suggest something quite different. "Slender" carries with it the feeling of being graceful and flexible. "Skinny" has a different feeling associated with it. "Skinny" carries with it the feeling of being undernourished, too thin, unhealthy. It is a much less positive word. When an author chooses a word, it is important to consider the shades of meaning.

When authors choose perfect words, they must also consider their **audience** and **purpose** for writing. Think for a minute about **audience**. Most people talk differently with their parents or teachers than they do with their friends. We tend to be more casual with friends and use slang or other more relaxed words. The same is true with authors. Authors write for a particular audience, and they select words that are appropriate for that audience. Word choice can be **formal** or **informal,** depending on the audience. If, for example, an author is writing an explanation of photosynthesis for students, the word choice will probably be formal, clear, and straightforward, using words with unambiguous meaning. If however, an author is writing a story with a narrator that directly talks to students, the word choice will be informal: chatty, lively, and relaxed.

Word choice also depends on the author's **purpose**. Authors have many different purposes for writing. The most common purposes for writing, though, are these: to entertain, to describe, to inform or explain, and to persuade or convince.

If authors are writing to entertain, they may use words that surprise, carry multiple meanings, and delight the reader. Authors may mix slang or colloquial language with more neutral or formal words to create the effect they are seeking. To describe, authors use vivid, exact words to help readers accurately experience a scene, process, or place. To inform, authors use clear, concrete words to impart information or explain a process. Finally, to persuade or convince, authors may use highly charged words to sway people's opinions. An author's words should always suit the audience and purpose of the piece.

Effective word choice gives freshness, originality, and precision to writing. When authors use words in surprising and unusual ways, they have the power to make people think, laugh, or examine new ideas. When authors use words in precise and technical ways, they have the power to help people understand difficult concepts. That's a gift and a responsibility.

Students in the elementary grades can learn to choose perfect words. They can learn to experiment and play with words. They can learn to examine words in the context of well-written passages and understand the power of choosing words that suit the audience and purpose. But it takes practice. That's what this chapter is about. These lessons will provide students with the tools they need in order to appreciate word choice in reading and to make appropriate and creative word choices in their own writing.

The lessons are designed to progress in difficulty in terms of both the text students analyze and the activities students participate in. However, it is certainly not necessary to use every lesson or to go in a particular order. In addition, each lesson's commentary and suggestions for teachers are exactly that: suggestions that you may or may not use in your work with students. You are the experts. You know your kids. Our intent is only to provide support for very busy professionals.

Of note are some threads that run through all of the Wonderful Words lessons. First, it is important that students be able to see the passages that form the foundation of each lesson. You can run off individual copies of the passages. You can also print them on chart paper or a whiteboard or project them. Another thread is the Wonderful Words Chart. This is a class chart of words and student-friendly definitions that students collect from the lessons' passages and activities. They should be words students find apt and appealing. There is a blank chart you can use at the end of this chapter on page 32. The third thread that runs through all of the lessons is a focus on purpose and audience. With each lesson, take a few minutes to be certain that students can answer these basic questions:

- What is the purpose of the passage?
- Who is the audience?
- What effect does this have on word choice?

You can keep a record of the purpose and audience of each passage and their effects in the chart on page 33 or on a large class chart. Finally, we have included additional practice with examples and nonexamples of how wonderful words improve writing. This practice can be found on pages 34–35.

We hope these lessons are engaging and helpful for you and your students. With practice, students can learn the power of wonderful words and go a long way toward finding their own voices.

Wonderful Words

Warm-up Lessons

The warm-up lessons are designed to introduce students to each element of voice. These lessons use simple text written to illustrate the specific element of voice under consideration—here, word choice. The questions direct students' attention to the purpose and power of understanding word choice in reading and using wonderful words in writing. In addition, we provide a brief review of the importance of word choice and suggest relevant academic language to include on word walls and in conversations with students.

Why word choice is important:
- The perfect word precisely expresses the feeling or idea an author wants to get across.
- Word choice reflects the author's purpose and audience.
- Effective word choice gives freshness, originality, and precision to writing.

Warm-up 1

> There once was a cat from D.C.
> That got his tail trapped in a tree.
> He finally got down
> But said with a frown,
> "This is not where I wanted to be!"
>
> > N. Dean

1. What is the purpose of the passage? (to entertain or amuse) Who is the audience? (anyone who loves words and funny poems)

2. What effect does this have on word choice? (Word choice is informal, reflecting the purpose and audience. Also, the rhyme scheme here affects word choice.)

3. Why does the author choose the word "trapped" instead of "caught"? ("Trapped" is stronger. It has the sense of being stuck with no way out. "Caught" is not as final and gives the reader the feeling that it is a brief problem.)

Warm-up 2

Hamsters are rodents. They are about six inches long, with short stubby tails and big cheeks. They vary in color from black to red to gold and often have a white stomach and black markings on the head and cheeks. Their eyes are black.

N. Dean

1. What is the purpose of the passage? (to inform or describe) Who is the audience? (people who want to know something about hamsters but don't have much knowledge about them)

2. What effect does this have on word choice? (Words are selected to clearly give information—the purpose—without slang or playful words. The words are also fairly simple, neutral, and designed for an audience with little background information.)

3. What does the word "stubby" add to the description? (lets the reader know hamsters' tails are not only short but also thick, giving a clearer picture of what hamsters look like.)

Word Wall Suggestions

author's purpose, audience, concrete, exact, persuade

Wonderful Words

Student Lesson 1

Consider the text:

We watch all the players who catch and who throw,

and the runners who **race** to each base down below.

Then, the **crack** of a bat — A home run! What a hit!

Look! The little ball **lands** in one lucky fan's mitt!

Michael Dahl, *Goodnight Baseball*

Take a deeper look:

1. Authors make lots of decisions when they write. They have to decide how to help you, the reader or listener, to get a picture in your mind of what is happening. One way to do this is to find a perfect word, a word that helps you understand exactly what is happening. What words in this passage help you see or hear exactly what is happening?

2. Which of these sentences is better at helping you understand what is happening? Why?

"Then, the **crack** of a bat — A home run! What a hit!"
or
"Then the bat hit the ball — A home run! What a hit!"

Now you try it:

Imagine that you and your friends are on the playground. Everyone is having fun, but it is almost time to go back to class. When the bell rings, the teacher calls the students back in. Imagine what the teacher sounds like when she calls the students in. Now think of a word that will help others understand exactly what the teacher sounds like. Complete the sentence with your word.

We hear all the students who play and who sing and the teacher who

_____ as the bell starts to ring.

Wonderful Words

Student Lesson 1

Commentary and Suggestions for Teachers

Lesson Objective: to find the perfect word that creates a particular picture

Consider the text:

Explain that *Goodnight Baseball* is about going to a baseball game and having a wonderful time. Then read the passage to students several times. As you read aloud, emphasize the boldface words.

Take a deeper look:

1. Start a Wonderful Words Chart with words from this passage that create a clear picture for the reader. As students suggest words from the passage, ask them to explain why they chose their word.

2. Read the two sentences aloud to students, and have them identify how the two sentences are different. Then have them discuss which one they like better and why. As they discuss the sentences, help them to see that "the crack of a bat" describes the scene more precisely than "the bat hit the ball," which is flat and somewhat boring. In any case, the bat is not doing the hitting—the baseball player is—with the bat. The second sentence does not give a clear picture of what is happening. "The crack of a bat" helps us clearly hear and picture the action.

Now you try it:

Read the sentence several times to students and have them talk about possible words in small groups or pairs. If they are stuck, give them suggestions such as "shouts," "screams," "roars," or "laughs." Let them have fun with words!

Wonderful Words

Student Lesson 2

Consider the text:

Amphibians have smooth, **moist** skin. Sometimes they **outgrow** their skin, and it **peels** off. This is called molting.

Isabel Martin, Amphibians: A Question and Answer Book

Take a deeper look:

1. Why do you think the author uses the word "moist" instead of "wet" to describe amphibians' skin?

2. Try to picture what it looks like when a frog "outgrows" its skin. Why does the skin "peel" off instead of "fall" off?

Now you try it:

Think of a pair of shoes you have outgrown. When they were too tight for you, how did you get them off? Act out what you did to get the shoes off. Now think of words like "peel" to describe what you did. Add these words to the Wonderful Words Chart.

Wonderful Words

Student Lesson 2

Commentary and Suggestions for Teachers

Lesson Objective: to choose the perfect word that creates a particular picture

Consider the text:

Read the passage aloud several times and write the boldface words in large letters for students to see. It would be useful to show them some pictures of typical amphibians, such as frogs, toads, and salamanders. Be sure students understand what each of the boldface words means. Compare the word "moist" to other words the author might have used, such as "wet" or "soggy." Help them begin to see how important it is for an author to choose the perfect word! They will be asked about this in question 1. Talk about the parts of the word "outgrow" and how we can figure out the meaning of words if we listen to them or look at them carefully. Then see if students can demonstrate what it means to peel something (they could peel a banana or peel off a sweater).

Take a deeper look:

1. An amphibian's skin isn't dripping with moisture. Rather, it is covered with a thin film of moisture. The word "wet" implies too much moisture and creates a false picture for the reader. "Moist" is the perfect word: not too wet and not too dry. Help students think of other things that could be moist rather than wet.

2. If the skin were to "fall" off, it would come off all at once. That's not what happens with an amphibian. As the amphibian grows, the animal rubs off the old skin gradually, making room for the new skin. The word "peel" captures this action, allowing the reader to picture a gradual unwrapping of the old skin to make way for the new.

Now you try it:

Divide students into small groups or pairs and have them act out taking off a very tight pair of shoes they have outgrown. Have them complete the sentence, "Sometimes they outgrow their shoes, and they have to _____ to get them off." Students could use words such as "pull," "yank," "tug," "jerk," "heave," or the like. Add their words to the Wonderful Words Chart.

Wonderful Words

Student Lesson 3

Consider the text:

Astrid was standing by the biggest and **gloomiest** castle she'd ever seen
…. Inside the castle, she found the Prince in a **deep, deep sleep**. He was
holding an empty silver cup.

"Was that a magic drink?" Astrid wondered. "If it was, I'll never wake him."
The Prince slept all night long.

Chris Powling, ***East of the Sun, West of the Moon***

Take a deeper look:

1. What does "gloomy" mean? Why do you think the author chose the word
"gloomiest" to describe the castle instead of "darkest"?

2. What is the difference between saying "deep, deep sleep" and just "deep sleep"?

Now you try it:

Close your eyes and try to imagine the most beautiful castle you can think of. Now
think of words you could use to describe this castle. Share your words with the
class and add some words to the Wonderful Words Chart.

Wonderful Words

Student Lesson 3

Commentary and Suggestions for Teachers

Lesson Objective: to use words that create a mood or feeling

Consider the text:

This passage is from a tale about the power of love. It is similar to ***Beauty and the Beast***—here the prince is a bear by day and a prince by night. Astrid helps her family by going to live with the bear. As the tale unfolds, Astrid makes a mistake and condemns the bear/prince to marry a terrible troll. Astrid travels great distances to save the prince, who is kept prisoner in the castle described in this passage. Of course the tale has a happy ending! Read the passage to students several times, stressing the boldface words.

Take a deeper look:

1. If students don't know what "gloomy" means, explain the word to them in student-friendly terms (like "shadowy," "sad," and "unhappy"). Let them talk about why the author describes the castle as the "gloomiest" castle instead of the "darkest" castle. They should come up with the idea that the word "gloomy" is much more specific and descriptive than "dark." It creates a mood or feeling. Something can be dark without being sad. But "gloomy" means both dark and sad. It is a more powerful, complex word and creates a clearer picture in the reader's mind.

2. The repetition of the word "deep" is for emphasis. It helps the reader understand how completely asleep the prince was. Only a magic drink could make the prince sleep that heavily! So Astrid is up against the magic of the troll, and the prince must be saved by something even more powerful: Astrid's love. At this point it would be fun to have students describe a few other things by repeating the adjectives. They could play with these phrases:

> sweet chocolate bar
> cold milk
> warm bed
> hungry dog

Now you try it:

If students have trouble imagining a castle, show them pictures of famous castles (both animated and actual). Then encourage students to come up with specific words that help their classmates understand exactly what the beautiful castle they are thinking of is like. Here are some words that could get them started: "peaceful," "happy," "glowing," "shining," "radiant," "joyful," "elegant." Note that these words create a mood as well as describe the castle. Write some of their words on the Wonderful Words Chart.

Wonderful Words

Student Lesson 4

Consider the text:

Dodos made nests on the ground. Females laid a single egg.
Dodos were **watchful** mothers.

Melissa Higgins, *Dodos*

Take a deeper look:

1. If you **watch** TV, you pay attention. If a soldier keeps **watch**, he is looking out for enemies. What do you think a "watchful" mother does? Draw a picture of a watchful mother bird.

2. Which sentence helps you have a better idea of what the dodo mother is like?

"Dodos were watchful mothers."

or

"Dodos were good mothers."

Now you try it:

Think about this sentence:

"Gabriella is a good dancer."

With your class, brainstorm all of the things that "good" could mean. Think carefully about what specific words you could use instead of "good" to describe how well Gabriella dances. Now choose which words or phrases are the most exact when it comes to Gabriella's dancing. Add some of your words to the Wonderful Words Chart.

Wonderful Words

Student Lesson 4

Commentary and Suggestions for Teachers

Lesson Objective: to find the perfect word that says exactly what the author wants to say

Consider the text:

This passage is from a book that describes what we know about dodos, which are extinct, flightless birds. Read the passage to students several times. Be certain they know what a nest is and understand that birds lay eggs instead of giving birth to live young.

Take a deeper look:

1. Answers will vary, but students should get the idea that the mother dodo carefully protected the eggs (and later her young) in her nest, keeping dangers away. The pictures should reflect the watchfulness of the mother dodo. It is not important that students know what a dodo looked like, but if you wish to share pictures of dodos, you can easily find images on the Internet.

2. The first sentence gives the reader (or listener) a much clearer picture of the mother dodo's behavior. A "good" mother could mean many things: kind, sympathetic, helpful, and so on. "Watchful" gives us a precise idea of what the dodo mother was like: on guard and protective. Authors try to find the exact word to focus the reader's attention on important ideas.

Now you try it:

Have students brainstorm words that could replace "good" in the sentence to give a more precise idea of what Gabriella is like as a dancer. Then have students select the word or phrase that they think most precisely describes the way Gabriella dances. Suggestions may include such words as "graceful," "skilled," "lively," "expert," and "experienced." Add some of their words to the Wonderful Words Chart.

Wonderful Words

Student Lesson 5

Consider the text:

In the gulley, a buffalo **looms**,

a bull with a head the size of a boulder.

His great black haunches sway slowly

from side to side as he **lumbers** toward the creek.

A thick ebony horn sprouts from each

side of his bulging brow. As he turns

one last time to watch us go, his eyes, each

larger than a cupped palm, are warm and sad.

Connie Colwell Miller, "Visiting the Buffalo" from Thorns, Horns, and Crescent Moons:
Reading and Writing Nature Poems

Take a deeper look:

1. Poets pay particular attention to words and look for the best possible words to create the experience of the poem. Of particular importance are action words, or verbs. This poem contains several precise verbs that help the reader fully understand the experience of the poem. Fill out the following chart to help you understand the exact meaning of "looms" in this poem.

to loom

Dictionary meaning	Meaning in your own words	Examples of other things that can "loom"

Why do you think the poet chose the word "looms" to describe the appearance of the buffalo?

2. "To lumber" means to move with a heaviness or clumsiness (another example of a precise verb). Have you ever seen a buffalo walk? If not, try to find a video of a buffalo walking. Does the buffalo "lumber"? Does the poet capture the movement of the buffalo with this word?

Now you try it:

Think of a hummingbird and the way it moves. With a partner, think of as many words as you can to capture the way a hummingbird moves. Choose your best word and use it to complete the sentence below.

The hummingbird searches for food as she _____ from flower to flower.

Now, with your partner, choose one of the animals below or another animal you are very familiar with and write an original sentence about how the animal moves. Use words that are clear, concrete, and exact to capture the movement.

chipmunk, sloth, jellyfish, horse, spider, elephant, caterpillar

Wonderful Words

Student Lesson 5

Commentary and Suggestions for Teachers

Lesson Objective: to capture the perfect word that describes an experience and creates a picture

Consider the text:

Read the poem aloud and ask students what they picture in their heads as you read it. Then call on several students to read the poem aloud again. Repeated readings should help students fully understand and experience the poem. It would be helpful to show some pictures of a buffalo and a video showing a buffalo walking. You can find pictures and videos readily on the Internet.

Take a deeper look:

1. Charts should look something like this:

to loom

Dictionary meaning	Meaning in your own words	Examples of other things that can "loom"
to appear in a large, strange, or frightening form, often in a sudden way (Merriam-Webster *Learner's Dictionary*)	to see something really big and kind of scary come into view all of a sudden	a test a punishment going back to school after a great vacation a thief a bully a bear

A buffalo is a huge, heavy animal. When you see one in the wild, it is startling. The buffalo does, indeed, loom into view. The poet has captured the perfect word for this experience.

2. A buffalo can lumber when he is not in a hurry, but a buffalo can also move quickly, even attack or stampede. Here the poet is describing the buffalo as it moves slowly and heavily toward the creek. The poet captures a specific movement in a specific time. Her attention to finding the perfect word produces the picture she wants to share with the reader.

Now you try it:

If students are unfamiliar with hummingbirds, show them a video of a hummingbird feeding, readily available on the Internet. To complete the sentence, students should come up with words like these: "flit," "dart," "hover," "dash," "flutter," "whiz." Then give students time to write their own sentences about the way another animal moves. Once they have completed their sentences, have them share them with the class. Add particularly good words to the Wonderful Words Chart.

Wonderful Words

Student Lesson 6

Consider the text:

Most peasants bathed once a week at most. They bathed in water from nearby streams where they also **dumped** sewage and trash. The water used for laundry was just as nasty. Peasants wore the same stiff, itchy clothes day in and day out.

> Kathy Allen, *The Horrible, Miserable Middle Ages: The Disgusting Details about Life During Medieval Times*

Take a deeper look:

1. In the second sentence, the author could have chosen to write, "They bathed in water from nearby streams where they also **put** sewage and trash." Instead she wrote, "They bathed in water from nearby streams where they also **dumped** sewage and trash." Why do you think she chose the word "dumped" instead of "put"?

2. Read the fourth sentence again. Now draw a picture of what you think the clothes looked like. What words in the fourth sentence are most important in helping you visualize the clothes?

Now you try it:

Pretend it is a bad day in the cafeteria. You have been served something shapeless and tasteless, and you're not even sure what it is. Write a sentence describing the food on your tray. Choose words that help the reader vividly experience what you describe. Use sentence four from *The Horrible, Miserable Middle Ages* as a model.

Wonderful Words

Student Lesson 6

Commentary and Suggestions for Teachers

Lesson Objective: to use words to create a clear, concrete, and exact picture for the audience

Consider the text:

This passage is from a lively book about the Middle Ages. It describes how dirty, dangerous, and uncomfortable life was at that time. It would be helpful to give students a little background knowledge about the Middle Ages before they read this passage: how long ago it was (between AD 500 and 1500); where the events of the Middle Ages took place (mainly Europe); and how the people lived. (dirty conditions, poverty, no sewage system or running water, no electricity, certainly no TV, cell phones, or computers. It was also the time of the bubonic plague, a terrible disease that killed more than one-third of the population of Europe.) Once they understand the context of this quote, read the quote aloud and then have a student or two read it again. Students should have fun with this lesson. They seem to love being grossed out, and this should do the trick!

Take a deeper look:

1. The word "dumped" is much stronger than the word "put." When you put something somewhere, you set it down or place it. It seems more careful. When you dump something, on the other hand, you toss it out. You get rid of something you don't want. It's a strong, careless action. You don't place sewage and trash carefully in a stream; you get rid of it, quickly and sloppily. The author used the exact word she needed to create a clear picture for the reader.

2. Students' pictures will vary, but most will focus on things sticking out of the clothes that make them stiff and itchy. They could also show trash stuck to the clothes. The words that are most important in helping students visualize the clothes are "sewage," "trash," "stiff," and "itchy." In sharing students' pictures, emphasize the importance of strong verbs (here, "dumped"). Sewage and trash are not just put in the water. They are dumped, giving a feeling of careless neglect.

Now you try it:

Students' sentences should be full of clear, concrete, and exact words, words that bring the reader into the experience. Have students share their sentences and add words to the Wonderful Words Chart.

Wonderful Words

Student Lesson 7

Consider the text:

She ran only to make herself warm, and she hated the wind which **rushed** at her face and **roared** and **held her back** as if it were some giant she could not see. **But** the big breaths of rough fresh air blown over the heather filled her lungs with something which was good for her whole thin body and whipped some red color into her cheeks and brightened her dull eyes when she did not know anything about it.

Frances Hodgson Burnett, The Secret Garden

Take a deeper look:

1. Look at the way the author describes the wind in the first sentence. Why do you think the girl, Mary, "hated the wind"?

2. At the beginning of the second sentence is a transition word: "But." The word "but" is used to introduce something different from what was just said. In the first sentence, Mary hates the wind; the different idea that follows the transition word "but" is that the wind is good for her. Fill in the following chart with words that show that the wind is disagreeable and words that show that the wind is good for her.

Words that show that the wind is disagreeable	Words that show that the wind is good for Mary

Now you try it:

Think about a task you don't like (doing the dishes, taking out the garbage, making your bed, cleaning your room, or something like that). Write one sentence that uses strong words to capture the unpleasantness of the task. Use Burnett's passage as a model. Start your sentence like this:

I hated _____

which _____

_____

Now write a second sentence starting with the word "But." This sentence should introduce something different from what was just said, some reason that task is important or valuable to do. Start your sentence like this:

But I do it because _____

_____

_____

_____

Wonderful Words

Student Lesson 7

Commentary and Suggestions for Teachers

Lesson Objective: to write about contrasting ideas using clear word choices

Consider the text:

This excerpt from *The Secret Garden* is the beginning of Mary's transformation from a skinny, sour child to a happy and healthy one. She is transformed through the power of friendship, exercise, and the garden. Read the passage several times to students. If you have time, it might be fun to have a discussion about whether students think a person can change without even realizing she is changing.

Take a deeper look:

1. The girl (Mary) sees nothing but the negative aspects of the wind. The wind "rushed," "roared," and "held her back." The words focus only on the wind as an enemy, even comparing the wind to an invisible giant. The wind is an opposing force, hated and resisted.

2. Charts should look something like this:

Words that show that the wind is disagreeable	Words that show that the wind is good for Mary
She ran only to make herself warm	big **breaths**
she **hated** the wind	rough **fresh** air
[the wind] **rushed** at her face	blown over the **heather**
[the wind] **roared**	**filled her lungs** with something which was
[the wind] **held her back**	**good for her whole thin body**
as if [the wind] were some **giant** she could not	**whipped** some **red color** into her cheeks
see	and **brightened** her dull eyes

Now you try it:

Sentences should look something like this:

I hated washing dishes, which coated my hands with slimy soap and stole time away from controlling my favorite video game character as he got to the next level. But I do it because I love it when my mom's face lights up if I do a chore without complaining.

Of course sentences will vary a lot. Have students share their work and pay particular attention to the two contrasting ideas and clear word choice to express both ideas.

To reinforce the transformation in thought, it would be helpful to have students volunteer to read their passages aloud, emphasizing with their choice of words and their voices the two contrasting ideas.

Wonderful Words

Student Lesson 8

Consider the text:

In its final stage of descent, the vehicle was suddenly **enveloped** in a thick cloud of moon dust, kicked up by the lunar module's exhaust system. Visibility was so poor that it was almost impossible to tell how close the moon's surface was. Nevertheless, with just 20 seconds of fuel left, the spacecraft set down without a hitch. It landed in a place called the Sea of Tranquility. When the engine was shut off, the dust immediately settled, clearing the view. Beyond Eagle's windows lay the barren surface of an **alien** world.

Pamela Dell, *Man on the Moon: How a Photograph Made Anything Seem Possible*

Take a deeper look:

1. This passage is about the first moon landing. Notice that people who write informational text use words as carefully and precisely as people who write stories. For example, read the first sentence several times and notice the word "enveloped." Why would the author use the word "enveloped" instead of a more common word like "covered"?

2. The view from the lunar module (named Eagle) is described as "the barren surface of an alien world." Why did the author use "alien" instead of "strange"? Think about the exact picture you get in your mind because of this word.

Now you try it:

Write a paragraph describing a time you watched a beautiful sunset or a rainbow. Use words that are clear, concrete, and exact to help your reader fully "see" and understand the experience.

Wonderful Words

Student Lesson 8

Commentary and Suggestions for Teachers

Lesson Objective: to express an idea using words that create a strong picture

Consider the text:

Have students read the passage silently several times, and then ask them to identify the topic and purpose of the passage. The topic is, of course, the first lunar landing. The purpose is to describe the landing so that readers fully understand what it was like and how it affected the astronauts and the people who heard about it (and saw pictures of it) at the time.

Take a deeper look:

1. When something is enveloped, it is completely encircled. It's like putting something in an envelope and sealing it. It is completely enclosed on all sides. When something is covered, it does not have the same impact. It doesn't have the same feeling of darkness, of being closed in and sealed. The moon dust doesn't just cover the vehicle. It engulfs it in darkness and surrounds it in a thick cloud; in short, the dust **envelops** the vehicle and makes it impossible to see.

2. The word "alien" creates a stronger picture than calling the world of the moon "strange." "Alien" brings with it the sense of otherworldliness, of being extraterrestrial (which, of course, it was). Things can be strange without being completely unfamiliar. But this world is **alien**, absolutely unfamiliar and foreign.

Now you try it:

First, have students describe, in their own words, a time they actually watched a sunset or saw a rainbow. Students should describe what they saw and what they were feeling. It is important to remind them that they will find more perfect words if they describe a tangible experience: something they actually saw. Then help students use a dictionary or thesaurus to find the best possible words and replace any bland or general words in the original description. Have students read the two versions of their descriptions and discuss how using a dictionary or a thesaurus can help them be better authors.

Wonderful Words

Student Lesson 9

Consider the text:

Soda ... is just **empty** calories. Sugar is a carbohydrate, but food with added sugar, such as soda and some fruit juices, is mostly sugar and no nutrients. They fill you with **"empty"** calories. The sugar in these drinks may give you a burst of energy. But then you'll **"crash"** and feel **sluggish** and **dizzy** in the middle of your game.

Dana Meachen Rau, *Sports Nutrition for Teen Athletes: Eat Right to Take Your Game to the Next Level*

Take a deeper look:

1. Food with added sugar is described as having "empty" calories, providing energy but no nutritional value. Why do you think the author uses the term "empty" calories rather than just saying "the food has sugar and no nutrients"?

2. Read the last sentence again. What does it mean to "crash" in the middle of a game? See if you can act out what the author means when she uses the word "crash." How would it change your understanding of the passage if the last sentence had been written like this?

"But then you might not feel very well in the middle of your game."

Now you try it:

Fill in the blanks with the word choices listed below the sentence.

The calcium in milk helps make your bones strong. You'll feel _____ and _____ as you get older.

sturdy	rugged
powerful	healthy
strong	fit
tough	

Wonderful Words

Student Lesson 9

Commentary and Suggestions for Teachers

Lesson Objective: to use strong and exact words to persuade or convince

Consider the text:

This is a great example of how authors of informational text select words carefully. It is also a great example of an informational text that sets out to persuade or convince the reader of a certain point of view. Here the author uses strong and exact words to convince readers not to drink soda. Have students read the passage several times (or read it to them). Emphasize that the author takes a solid stand against soda and other sugary drinks, and that she communicates her stand through careful word choice ("empty," "crash," "sluggish," "dizzy").

Take a deeper look:

1. Calling the calories "empty" is much stronger than simply saying that sugary drinks have no nutrients. Using the word "empty" creates the sense of hollowness or even meaninglessness. Sugary drinks "fill you with empty calories." In other words, you are full and empty at the same time. The calories provide no lasting value.

2. The author defines "crash" in the sentence as becoming "sluggish" and "dizzy" after a burst of energy. If students don't understand that the word "crash" is defined for them in the sentence, help them to notice the clues (the use of the word "but" after the burst of energy to indicate a contrary idea; explaining how you'll feel if you crash). It would be fun to call on students to act this out. The rewritten sentence loses all of its power and specificity. Not feeling well could be caused by anything—a cold, the flu, something you ate. Crashing (in this sentence) specifically refers to what happens when you are very active after the brief burst of energy you get after drinking a sugary drink. The word is clear, concrete, and exact.

Now you try it:

There are many ways students could complete this sentence, but students' sentences should look something like this:

The calcium in milk helps make your bones strong. You'll feel sturdy and powerful as you get older.

Wonderful Words

Student Lesson 10

Consider the text:

A **loud murmur** goes through the crowd as a soldier with a full beard steps out onto the balcony of the Ashton Villa.

"That must be old Granger," says Sam.

The crowd grows **silent** as General Granger begins to read from a paper in his hands. Your ears tingle when he reads the words:

"The people of Texas are informed that in accordance with a proclamation from the Executive of the United States, all slaves are free."

Steven Otfinoski, The Story of Juneteenth: An Interactive History Adventure

Take a deeper look:

1. A "murmur" is a low, quiet sound. How can the murmur in this passage be loud?

2. An author chooses his or her words carefully in order to make the reader feel a certain way. For example, this author says, "The crowd grows silent as General Granger begins to read from a paper in his hands." Think about the word "silent." Why does the author choose the word "silent" instead of the word "quiet"?

Now you try it:

Think about a very hot day. You have been outside riding your bicycle or running around and are very hot and sweaty. Now you are going inside where it is cool and there is a glass of cold lemonade ready for you. Complete the following sentence with the best word possible to help others understand exactly how you moved when you went inside.

I was hot and thirsty from my morning outside. The sun was burning down, and even the wind was steamy. My brother called from inside to tell me that I had a glass of cold lemonade waiting for me. I _____ inside.

Wonderful Words

Student Lesson 10

Commentary and Suggestions for Teachers

Lesson Objective: to capture a feeling or idea with perfect words

Consider the text:

Have students read the passage to themselves (or read it aloud to them) several times, looking for words they think create a perfect picture for the reader. If they have copies of the passage, they can underline or circle those words. If not, they can write down the words. Then read the passage aloud again, emphasizing the boldface words. Have students share the words they selected and explain why they chose the words.

Take a deeper look:

1. A murmur is quiet; but here it is the murmur of a crowd, so there are lots of murmurs together, creating a loud but low noise. By using the words "loud murmur," the author creates a vivid experience for the reader: the sense of hushed talking, private and almost secretive, and the communal experience of everyone murmuring at once. It creates a clear sense of both eagerness and hesitation.

2. The word "silent" creates a totally different feeling than does the word "quiet." "Quiet" is a neutral word, a word that doesn't have strong feelings associated with it. "Quiet" simply means there is little noise around. "Silent," though, indicates complete soundlessness. A silent crowd is completely still, without noise or movement. There is a hushed feeling of anticipation. The author has chosen the perfect word for the effect he wants to create.

Now you try it:

Students should try to find the perfect word to capture how they moved inside. "Ran" is OK, but they can assuredly do much better. If they are stuck, give them a few suggestions to get them started ("tore," "scampered," "darted," "slid," etc.). It might also be a good time to bring out the thesaurus and help students discover perfect words. To reinforce the value of the thesaurus, students can compare their sentences before and after using the thesaurus and discuss the impact of finding the perfect word. Have students share their words with the class and add them to the Wonderful Words Chart.

Wonderful Words

Student Lesson 11

Consider the text:

Then the Cyclops in his **wrath** broke off the top of a great hill, a mighty rock, and **hurled** it where he had heard the voice. Right in front of the ship's bow it fell, and a great wave rose as it sank, and washed the ship back to the shore. But Ulysses **seized** a long pole with both hands and pushed the ship from the land and bade his comrades ply their oars, nodding with his head, for he was too wise to speak, lest the Cyclops should know where they were. Then they rowed with all their might and main.

"The Cyclops," *Myths and Legends of All Nations*, translated and edited by Logan Marshall

Take a deeper look:

1. This passage is from the story of how Ulysses (also known as Odysseus) escapes from the Cyclops, a one-eyed monster that has held Ulysses and his men captive in a cave. In this passage, Ulysses and his men escape through cleverness and trickery and Ulysses makes fun of the Cyclops. Ulysses and his men almost get caught again, but they do escape. Look at the first sentence again. What does "wrath" mean? Look it up if you don't know the word and be sure you understand the definition. Is the word "wrath" stronger or weaker than "anger"? Defend your answer.

2. There are two very strong verbs (action words) in this passage: "hurled" and "seized." How do these verbs help you clearly understand what is happening in the passage? How would it change your understanding of the passage if we substituted "threw" for "hurled" and "took" for "seized"?

Now you try it:

Rewrite the following sentence using stronger verbs that help your reader clearly understand what is happening. The verbs are underlined to help you identify them.

Lucy <u>hit</u> the ball and <u>ran</u> to first base.

Wonderful Words

Student Lesson 11

Commentary and Suggestions for Teachers

<u>Lesson Objective:</u> to create a concrete picture using strong verbs

Consider the text:

Sharing background information would be helpful before reading this passage. This is a short passage from the adventures of Ulysses (his Latin name), also called Odysseus (his Greek name). The story, known commonly as **The Odyssey**, tells of Ulysses' journey from Troy at the end of the Trojan War until he makes it home to Greece. The conflict with the Cyclops is one of his many adventures. This passage has several uncommon words that may give students trouble: "bade" (past tense of "bid," to ask), "ply" (use, as in "apply"), "lest" (in case), "main" (strongest purpose). You might want to read a simplified version of the whole story to students as an enrichment activity. Once students have some background, read the passage several times and go over any words they are unfamiliar with.

Take a deeper look:

1. The word "wrath" means great, often vengeful, anger. As such, it is stronger than the word "anger."

2. The strong verbs in this passage intensify the action and help the reader clearly understand what is going on. If we substituted "threw" for "hurled," the sentence would lose its power. To "throw" could be weak and nonthreatening. But to "hurl" something is to place power and precision behind the action. It presents a clear threat. In the same way, there is no power in "taking" a long pole. It is a simple action that has no urgency or strength. The verb "seize," on the other hand, has the feeling of purposeful action, strong and immediate.

Now you try it:

There are many verbs students could use to substitute for the weak verbs in this sentence. Here are some examples:

Instead of "hit": "slugged," "bashed," "belted," "whacked," "smashed," "shattered"

Instead of "ran": "jetted," "sprinted," "raced," "tore," "slid," "scampered"

This would be a good time to have students look back at their own writing and replace some of their old, abstract words with stronger and more exact words.

Wonderful Words

Student Lesson 12

Consider the text:

On the evening of March 5, 1770, a **mob** of angry colonists began insulting a British guard standing in front of a customs house in Boston. The crowd **pelted** him with snowballs and sticks. Eight other British soldiers soon came to the soldier's rescue. In the confusion the soldiers opened fire without their captain's command. Five colonists were killed. Others were injured. Patriots blamed the British soldiers for the tragedy, which became known as the "Boston Massacre."

Kassandra Radomski, *Battle for a New Nation: Causes and Effects of the Revolutionary War*

Take a deeper look:

1. What is a mob? How is a mob different from a crowd? Why do you think the author used the word "mob" here?

2. Read the second sentence of this passage again. What does it mean to pelt someone? If you don't know the word, look it up in the dictionary. Be certain you understand the definition and can put the definition into your own words. Explain how the effect of the sentence would be different if the author had written it like this:

"The crowd threw snowballs and sticks at him."

Now you try it:

Think about a time you did something you were very proud of. Perhaps you scored the winning run in a baseball or softball game or received a very good grade on a test. Now picture your family or friends being very proud of you (which makes you happy) and complete the sentence below by filling in the blank. Be certain your word creates a positive feeling for the reader. Be creative! Add your perfect word to the class Wonderful Words Chart.

My family (or friends) _____ me with smiles and praise.

Wonderful Words

Student Lesson 12

Commentary and Suggestions for Teachers

<u>Lesson Objective:</u> to describe an event precisely with clear, concrete, and exact words

Consider the text:

Read the passage aloud several times. Then ask students to discuss the action described in the passage. They are able to do this because the words are clear, concrete, and exact.

Take a deeper look:

1. A crowd is simply a group of people gathered together. The word does not suggest the mood of the gathering. A mob, on the other hand, suggests an angry, disorderly gathering of people. The author uses "mob" instead of "crowd" in this sentence to suggest the mood of the colonists: angry and out of control.

2. To pelt someone is to repeatedly hurl something at or hit someone with repeated force. Here the word helps the reader understand that the colonists were getting out of hand, losing control. If the author had written, "The crowd threw snowballs and sticks at him," the sentence would lack impact and precision. It might almost sound harmless, especially when associated with "snowballs," which are often thrown in fun. Using the word "pelt" helps the reader understand that there was nothing fun about this. The Patriots were angry and quite serious.

Now you try it:

The words students choose should create a positive picture. They could use such words as these: "showered," "covered," "surrounded," "circled." Have students share their sentences with a partner or the class and add some of their words to the Wonderful Words Chart. Be certain that students use words with the correct connotation. If they use words such as "bombarded" or "drowned," they will create the feeling that the smiles and praise were overwhelming—not a pleasant experience. If students don't understand this, divide the class into two groups. Have group one use words that indicate being overwhelmed or embarrassed about the smiles and praise (words like "smothered" or "attacked"). Have group two use words that indicate comfort and pleasure with the smiles and praise. A lively discussion will help students understand the importance of the perfect word and how words help them create the effect they want to their readers to experience.

Additional Resources for Wonderful Words

Wonderful Words Chart

Words We Love	What the Words Mean

Words, Purpose, and Audience

Questions to ask with every lesson:
- What is the purpose of the passage?
- Who is the audience?
- What effect does this have on word choice?

Keep a class record of the purpose, audience, and effect on word choice in each lesson. The chart will help students understand the importance of word choice and how word choice is connected to the author's purpose and the audience of any particular text.

Lesson #	Purpose	Audience	Effect on Word Choice
1			
2			
3			
4			
5			
6			
7			
8			
9			
10			
11			
12			

Examples and Nonexamples

Students can examine the text samples below to see the importance of choosing precise words in their writing. These examples and nonexamples allow students to

- experience how words help the reader identify what is important,
- compare the different levels of word choice using evidence to explain which example is the best, and
- look at their own writing and see what they need to do to make the writing come alive with perfect words.

Have students read all three examples and then use the chart to rank the passages' use of words and explain why purposeful word choice is essential to quality writing.

Summer with Grandma by N. Danaher

Ex. 1: I had a really great summer. I went to my grandma's house for a whole month. She lives in Ohio.

Ex. 2: My summer was really nice because I stayed with my grandma.

Ex. 3: Summer had just started when I found out I'd be torn from my friends to be with my grandma for a month. I was furious at my parents. How could they condemn me to a month in Ohio? Ohio was five long hours away, and I was going to miss conquering the terrifying new water slide at my summer camp. But as we pulled into her endless driveway, she was standing there to welcome me. Her smile stretched from ear to ear and I smelled her signature chocolate chip cookies baking. I couldn't be mad anymore. I knew that I was in the right place. The water slide would just have to wait.

General Words	Some Specific Words	Precise Words
Example number:	Example number:	Example number:
Why it doesn't work:	Why it's better but still not great:	Why it's the best:

Whiskers by N. Danaher

Ex. 1: My mom's face was somber, and I knew what she was about to say wouldn't make me happy. "Whiskers is dead," she said, and my throat instantly hardened like water in an ice tray. Whiskers was my little gerbil, my first pet, and a part of the family. I threw my arms around my mom and gripped her waist as hard as I could. She couldn't bring back Whiskers, but her hug was soothing and let me know that I would be OK.

Ex. 2: When my mom told me that my pet gerbil died, I was really sad.

Ex. 3: One of the saddest days of my life was when I lost my pet gerbil. She was my first pet, and I miss her a lot.

General Words	Some Specific Words	Precise Words
Example number:	Example number:	Example number:
Why it doesn't work:	Why it's better but still not great:	Why it's the best:

Dazzling Detail

Introduction

Detail is what makes writing come alive. Detail includes facts, observations, reasons, examples, and incidents—everything that an author uses to develop a main idea. It is important that students understand and distinguish between main idea and supportive details in both their reading and writing. Understanding the difference between main idea and detail helps them comprehend complex text and makes them clearer and more expressive writers.

Specific details create a strong mental picture for the reader by focusing on particulars rather than abstractions. In other words, instead of just saying, "I had a great time at the baseball game," authors fill their papers with the *specifics* of what made the game great. "A great time" means different things to different people. Exactly what made the game great? Was it fun being with parents or a sibling? Was the food sloppy but delicious? Was it a close, exciting game? Did someone hit a home run? Did a fan catch a ball someone hit into the stands? Students will get this idea with practice. Detail helps readers thoroughly understand the main idea and helps authors explain what they're writing about exactly as they want their readers to comprehend it.

Detail also helps to focus the reader's attention on important ideas and shapes the reader's understanding of a topic. For example, let's say a student wants to describe a camping trip. The student can't describe everything—that would make a boring and rambling essay. Instead, he or she has to decide what the main idea will be (the focus). The student could focus on the animals he or she saw while camping (for example, a deer, a raccoon, a bear, a fox); the scenery (for example, snowcapped mountains, valleys filled with wildflowers, a river or stream); or how uncomfortable it was sleeping on the ground. Having a clear focus will help students select appropriate details.

Focus is also determined by the attitude the author wants to convey. Maybe the author's attitude is that camping is relaxing and peaceful, or maybe he or she wants to express discomfort with the rain, cold, wet firewood, and insects. The author decides. And once an author decides, he or she selects the details that support, develop, and enliven both focus and attitude. If students do it like the experts, the detail they select will guide their readers into the experience in just the way they want. They get to choose how their readers experience camping! Details allow the reader to participate as an equal partner in the "world" the author has created and to follow the author's ideas in the way the writer intends.

Students in the elementary grades can learn to distinguish between main idea (focus) and detail. They can improve their comprehension of complex text by identifying the author's focus and attitude and how the author supports his or her focus and reveals his or her attitude through the choice of detail. They can also become better authors themselves by determining their own focus and attitude and building paragraphs or stanzas through concrete detail. But it takes practice. That's what this chapter is about. These lessons will provide students with the tools they need in order to understand the relationship between main ideas and detail in reading and to make good decisions about main ideas and detail in their own writing.

The lessons are designed to progress in difficulty in terms of both the text students analyze and the activities students participate in. However, it is certainly not necessary to use every lesson or to go in a particular order. In addition, each lesson's commentary and suggestions for teachers are exactly that: suggestions that you may or may not use in your work with students. You are the experts. You know your kids. Our intent is only to provide support for very busy professionals.

Of note are some threads that run through all of the Dazzling Detail lessons. First, it is important that students be able to see the passages that form the foundation of each lesson. You can run off individual copies of the passages. Alternatively, you can print them on chart paper or a whiteboard or project them. Another thread is the Dazzling Detail Chart. This is a class chart in which students can list the topic, main idea or focus, details, and how the details from the lessons' passages help you understand the main idea. There is a blank chart you can use at the end of this chapter on page 68. The third thread that runs through all of the lessons is an emphasis on the basics of main idea and detail. With each lesson, take a few minutes to be certain that students can answer these basic questions:

- What is the main idea of the passage?
- What are the details that support the main idea?
- How do the details help you understand the main idea?

You can keep a record of the main idea and details of each passage in the chart on page 68. With practice, students will master these skills. Finally, we have included additional practice with examples and nonexamples of how dazzling detail improves writing. This practice can be found on pages 69–70.

We hope these lessons are engaging and helpful for you and your students. With practice, students can learn the power of dazzling detail and go a long way toward finding their own voices.

Dazzling Detail

Warm-up Lessons

The warm-up lessons are designed to introduce students to each element of voice. These lessons use simple text written to illustrate the specific element of voice under consideration—here, detail. The questions direct students' attention to the purpose and power of understanding detail in reading and using detail in writing. In addition, we provide a brief review of the importance of detail and suggest relevant academic language to include on word walls and in conversations with students.

Why detail is important:
- Detail creates strong mental images for the reader.
- Detail helps focus the reader's attention on important ideas.
- Detail conveys the author's attitude.
- Detail shapes the reader's understanding of a topic.

Warm-up 1

Violet woke up early on Saturday. It was the start of a wonderful day. The sun made the drops from last night's rain sparkle on the grass. A bird landed on her windowsill and sang its little heart out. Violet smelled her mother's blueberry muffins baking downstairs.

N. Dean

1. What is the main idea of the passage? (It was the start of a wonderful day.)

2. What details support the main idea? (Violet woke up early. The rain was sparkling on the grass. The bird was singing on her windowsill. Blueberry muffins were baking downstairs.)

3. How do these details help you understand the main idea? (They make the general, abstract idea of a wonderful day focused and specific. The details also reveal the attitude, which is positive, happy, and anticipatory.)

Warm-up 2

Many people think that spiders are insects, but spiders are not insects. All spiders have eight legs. Insects never have more than six legs. No spider has wings. Many insects have wings and can fly. Baby spiders look like tiny versions of adult spiders. Baby insects look completely different from adult insects.

> T. W. Dean

1. What is the main idea of the passage? (Spiders are not insects.)

2. What details support the main idea? (Spiders have eight legs; insects have six legs. Spiders have no wings; most insects have wings and can fly. Baby spiders look like tiny adult spiders; baby insects do not look like the adult insects.)

3. How do these details help you understand the main idea? (The details "prove" the main idea. The details are examples of how spiders and insects are different, helping the reader understand that spiders and insects are definitely not the same.)

Word Wall Suggestions

abstract, concrete, specific, main idea, detail, attitude, stanza, point of view

Dazzling Detail

Student Lesson 1

Consider the text:

> Kids who use wheelchairs go many places. They use ramps to get into vans. They use ramps to enter and exit buildings. Kids who use wheelchairs go to the library. They read books and use computers.
>
> Lola M. Schaefer, **Some Kids Use Wheelchairs**

Take a deeper look:

1. What is the main idea of this passage? How do you know the main idea is true?

2. Think of as many details as you can from this passage, and tell them to another student. Why do you think the author uses all of these details?

Now you try it:

Let's start with a general statement:

I like to go to the playground.

Now think of all of the details you could add to that general statement to help others understand why you like the playground. With your class, compose four or five sentences. Your first sentence should be "I like to go to the playground." The other sentences should give details that you like about the playground.

Dazzling Detail

Student Lesson 1

Commentary and Suggestions for Teachers

Lesson Objective: to understand the connection between main idea and detail

Consider the text:

This book is focused on what students in wheelchairs **can** do. They go places, stretch their muscles, play sports, and go to camp. Read the passage several times aloud. Notice that the main idea is in the first sentence. Of course, that is not always true in text, but it is usually true in informational text designed for young students.

Take a deeper look:

1. The main idea is that kids who use wheelchairs go many places, stated in the first sentence. Have students say that sentence several times. Then ask them to answer the rest of the question: how they know the main idea to be true. Guide them in their discussion back to the passage and away from any personal experience they may have. The "proof" of the main idea lies in the details of the passage. Read the passage aloud until they can give you all of the details that support the main idea. (They use ramps, get into vans, get in and out of buildings, go to the library, read books, and use computers.) The vocabulary is important here, so it is best to use the words "main idea" and "detail," words that students can see on your word wall, so that students get accustomed to those terms.

2. Students should list the details in the passage: "They use ramps to get into vans. They use ramps to enter and exit buildings. Kids who use wheelchairs go to the library. They read books and use computers." The author uses the details to support the main idea and to help the reader fully understand the opening statement, "Kids who use wheelchairs go many places." Without the details, it would just be a general statement without the power to help readers fully understand content.

Now you try it:

Make a list of all of the details students come up with. Then turn the details into four or five sentences. Write them clearly for students to see. They can then practice reading the passage they have created.

Dazzling Detail

Student Lesson 2

Consider the text:

> Look for yellow when you're weary
>
> Smiling color makes you cheery
>
> Lemonade in hot July
>
> Flowers reaching for the sky
>
> Shining when you need a lift
>
> Nature's golden brightest gift

Laura Purdie Salas, "Sunshine," *Flashy, Clashy, and Oh-So Splashy: Poems about Color*

Take a deeper look:

1. What is the main idea of this poem? Which lines of the poem tell you the main idea?

2. What are the details that support the main idea?

Now you try it:

Think about your favorite color. What are some things that have your favorite color? For example, if my favorite color is blue, I might think of the sky, my cat's eyes, a shirt I like, or my lunch box. Talk about your favorite color with a partner. Now write a main idea and two sentences that give details about your main idea. You can make your favorite color sentences into a poem if you like!

Dazzling Detail

Student Lesson 2

Commentary and Suggestions for Teachers

<u>Lesson Objective:</u> to understand how details support the main idea and reveal the author's attitude

Consider the text:

This is a poem about the color yellow. The purpose is to entertain and give insight. The audience is young people (The vocabulary and rhythm are simple, and the poem is upbeat and full of concrete detail). Read the poem aloud several times. Be sure to clarify the vocabulary for students, especially "weary" (tired) and "cheery" (happy). Yellow is usually considered a happy color. It would be fun to discuss this with students and see if they can think of other yellow things that make them happy.

Take a deeper look:

1. The main idea is that things that are yellow will make you happy when you are tired or sad. The main idea is stated in lines one and two ("Look for yellow when you're weary / Smiling color makes you cheery").

2. The details that support the main idea are examples of happy things that are yellow: lemonade in summer and flowers such as sunflowers, which grow very tall toward the sun. It would be helpful to show students a picture of a field of sunflowers, readily available on the Internet.

Now you try it:

Give students time to think and talk about colors and colorful things. Then they can write a paragraph or a poem, modeled after the poem about yellow. Poems should look something like this:

Look for purple when you're cold.

It will make your heart feel bold.

Purple sunsets make me warm.

Purple curtains hide a storm.

A paragraph should look something like this:

I love the color purple. It makes me feel warm when I'm cold and makes me feel strong when I am afraid. For example, when I look at a purple sunset, I feel warm and comforted. When I close the purple curtains in my room, I feel safe when there is a storm outside.

Students should share their poems or paragraphs with the class.

Dazzling Detail

Student Lesson 3

Consider the text:

Volcanoes on the ocean floor formed the Hawaiian islands thousands of years ago. On the Big Island, active volcanoes still add new land to the island and make it bigger. At Hawaii Volcanoes National Park, red hot lava flows out of the ground down to the sea.

Mary Lindeen, ***Parks of the U.S.A.***

Take a deeper look:

1. What is the main idea of this paragraph? Be careful here! Sometimes the main idea is not directly stated.

2. Which details support the main idea?

Now you try it:

In boldface below is a main idea statement about dogs. Write two sentences that support the main idea. Remember to be as specific as you can. General details (such as "dogs are nice") are not as effective as specific details (such as "dogs keep you company when you go for a walk").

Dogs make good pets.

Dazzling Detail

Student Lesson 3

Commentary and Suggestions for Teachers

Lesson Objective: to understand the importance of specific details in focusing the reader's attention

Consider the text:

This is informational text. The purpose is to inform, and the audience is students. Read the passage several times aloud, and then have students read the passage silently. The topic, of course, is volcanoes in Hawaii but the main idea itself is not directly stated. This is fairly common in informational text. Figuring out the main idea will be good practice for students.

Take a deeper look:

1. The main idea (Volcanoes formed and are still forming the land in Hawaii) is not directly stated. Many students will think it is stated in the first sentence, but it is not. The first sentence is a detail. The rest of the paragraph is not about Hawaii thousands of years ago. The whole paragraph is about how volcanoes build the land in Hawaii. If students are stuck about the main idea, you can give them a multiple-choice option:

    a.   Volcanoes on the ocean floor formed the Hawaiian islands thousands of years ago.
    b.   Volcanoes are still active in Hawaii.
    c.   **Volcanoes formed and are still forming the land in Hawaii.**
    d.   The lava that comes from volcanoes is very hot.

2. Once students understand the main idea, it is easier to figure out the supporting details. Each sentence in the paragraph contains a supporting detail: Volcanoes on the ocean floor formed the Hawaiian islands thousands of years ago; active volcanoes still add new land to the Big Island; lava flows out of the ground toward the sea.

Now you try it:

Give students time to talk about this. They should focus on as many specific ways as they can think of that support the main idea (Dogs make good pets). This would be a good time for partner or group writing. Let students work together to write a specific, detailed paragraph about the ways dogs make good pets. Have students share their work.

Dazzling Detail

Student Lesson 4

Consider the text:

The Mole had been working very hard all morning, spring-cleaning his little home. First with brooms, then with dusters; then on ladders and steps and chairs, with a brush and a pail of whitewash; till he had dust in his throat and eyes, and splashes of whitewash all over his black fur, and an aching back and weary arms.

Kenneth Grahame, *The Wind in the Willows*

Take a deeper look:

1. What had the Mole been doing all morning? What details help you understand that Mole was working hard?

2. How would it change your understanding of the passage if the author had written it like this?

"The Mole had been working very hard all morning, spring-cleaning his little home. He cleaned his house and did a little painting. It was very tiring."

Now you try it:

Think of something you like to do—dancing, playing soccer, playing kickball, riding your bike, cooking—anything active you like to do. Complete the following sentence:

I had been _____ **all afternoon.**

Now think of all of the details about what you were doing all afternoon than would help someone else understand why you like this activity. Share your details with a partner and see if your partner can explain why you like this activity.

Dazzling Detail

Student Lesson 4

Commentary and Suggestions for Teachers

<u>**Lesson Objective:**</u> to understand how details create a clear picture for the reader

Consider the text:

The Mole, of course, is a character in the story. You might have to explain to students what a mole is and what spring-cleaning and whitewash (white paint) are. Read the passage aloud several times. It would be fun to call on a few students to act out what is happening as you read.

Take a deeper look:

1. Mole has been cleaning his home. The details that help the reader understand that Mole was working hard include the breathless way (one thing after another!) the author describes how he was cleaning ("with brooms, then with dusters; then on ladders and steps and chairs, with a brush and a pail of whitewash"); the effects of all of that cleaning (giving Mole "dust in his throat and eyes, and splashes of whitewash all over his black fur"); and how the work made Mole feel (giving him "an aching back and weary arms").

2. If the author had written the passage like the sentence below, it would lose all of its interest. The reader would not have a clear or specific idea of what Mole did in his cleaning or what it meant for Mole to be tired (dust in his throat and eyes, white paint on his fur, a sore back and tired arms). The general statements ("He cleaned his house and did a little painting. It was very tiring.") do not create a vivid picture in the reader's mind. Encourage students to be as specific as they can be when they use detail in their own oral language or writing.

"The Mole had been working very hard all morning, spring-cleaning his little home. He cleaned his house and did a little painting. It was very tiring."

Now you try it:

Write the sentence stem ("I had been _____ all afternoon.") on the board or chart paper and read it to students several times. Partner students up and have them do this exercise orally. Each student should name what he/she had been doing all afternoon. Then give them time to talk about it, stressing the importance of using specific detail to help their partner understand what they like about this activity. Call on some students to explain why their partner likes his or her activity. It is details that enable students to understand what is likable about their partner's activity.

Dazzling Detail

Student Lesson 5

Consider the text:

Ground sloths lived in North and South America during the Ice Age. They made their homes in caves, grasslands, and forests. Too big to climb trees, ground sloths lived on the ground. They walked on all fours with their clawed feet turned in. Ground sloths had shaggy fur and sharp claws. They stood on strong back legs to reach the leafy treetops. Thick tails helped them balance.

Joy Frisch-Schmoll, Ground Sloths

Take a deeper look:

1. Draw a picture of a ground sloth based on the paragraph below:

"Ground sloths are extinct animals that lived in North and South America a long time ago. They lived all over the place. They were very big. They could walk on all four feet or stand up on their back legs. They had tails."

2. Now read or listen to the paragraph describing ground sloths by Frisch-Schmoll. Read or listen to the paragraph several times, and then draw a picture of the ground sloth. Compare this picture to the one you drew from the description in question 1. Which picture is more specific and clear? Why do you think that is so?

Now you try it:

Write a paragraph about an animal you are very familiar with. It could be a pet or an animal you have seen in your yard, in the park, or in the zoo. Use lots of detail in your description so that anyone reading your paragraph could draw this animal. Exchange paragraphs with a partner and see if your partner can draw the animal from your description. You don't have to be an expert artist here! Just include all of the detail from the paragraph.

Dazzling Detail

Student Lesson 5

Commentary and Suggestions for Teachers

Lesson Objective: to understand how details focus the reader's attention and create a clear picture for the reader

Consider the text:

Read this passage after students have had a chance to hear the passage in question 1 and draw a picture. Comparing the abstract description in question 1 with the passage from ***Ground Sloths*** will help students understand the impact of specific detail on comprehension. The paragraph is an overall description of the sloth, describing the sloth's attributes (where it lived, what it looked like, some of its behavior). The details from ***Ground Sloths*** help focus the reader's attention on specifics. As you read the passage aloud, ask students to close their eyes and try to picture what the sloth looked like. Students can then read the passage themselves.

Take a deeper look:

1. It is almost impossible to draw a picture from this paragraph. There are no specific details! The writing is too general and abstract. What kind of background could they draw? How big is "big"? What did sloths' feet, legs, and tail look like? Encourage students to make the connection between providing specific detail in writing and being able to accurately comprehend what they are reading.

2. The second picture should be much more specific. That is because the paragraph provides a concrete and detailed description. Students' pictures should reflect the specific details of the paragraph: background (ice, caves, grassland, forests); size; sharp claws on turned-in feet; and shaggy fur. They can picture the sloth on all fours or standing on its back legs. Call on some students to share their pictures.

Now you try it:

You might want to have students think about or find a picture (from a magazine, the Internet, or an actual photo) of the animal for the previous night's homework. This way, no students are spending time thinking of what to write about. As they describe their animal, students should use lots of specific detail. For example, instead of saying a cat is furry, they could say that the cat left a trail of white hair on every piece of furniture in the house. Specific detail makes writing more alive and interesting. It also helps the reader fully understand what the author is trying to say. Students should have fun exchanging paragraphs and drawing the pictures. The more detail they use in their paragraphs, the more accurate the pictures will be.

If students have a writing notebook or portfolio, it would be helpful to have them look back at previous samples of writing and find opportunities to include specific detail. They don't have to do a major rewrite. It can be as simple as writing changes on a sticky note or in a different color pencil than their original writing. This practice will give students a chance to reflect on how they can use more detail in their writing.

Dazzling Detail

Student Lesson 6

Consider the text:

Then the little Hiawatha
Learned of every bird its language,
Learned their names and all their secrets,
How they built their nests in summer,
Where they hid themselves in winter,
Talked with them whene'er he met them,
Called them "Hiawatha's Chickens."

Of all beasts he learned the language,
Learned their names and all their secrets,
How the beavers built their lodges,
Where the squirrels hid their acorns,
How the reindeer ran so swiftly,
Why the rabbit was so timid,
Talked with them whene'er he met them,
Called them "Hiawatha's Brothers."

Henry W. Longfellow, "Hiawatha's Childhood"

Take a deeper look:

1. Read the first stanza several times. This stanza tells what Hiawatha learns from the birds. Which details show what Hiawatha learns from the birds?

2. Now read the second stanza several times. This stanza tells what Hiawatha learns from the "beasts" (the animals of the forest). Which details show what Hiawatha learns from the beasts? How do these details make the poem more interesting?

Now you try it:

Write a four-line poem using detail to show what you have learned from a pet or a wild animal. Use Longfellow's poem as a model. Part of the poem is done for you.

From a pet/wild animal_____ **I learned its secrets,**
(name the animal)

How_____ ,

Where _____ ,

Why_____ .

Dazzling Detail

Student Lesson 6

Commentary and Suggestions for Teachers

Lesson Objective: to understand the difference between abstract description and concrete detail

Consider the text:

Hiawatha was a great Native American leader who lived a long time ago. Many stories and poems have been written about him. These two stanzas tell about the things Hiawatha learns when he is a child. Read the stanzas aloud several times, paying attention to the sounds and rhythm of the poem. The poem creates strong mental pictures for the reader through the use of details. Some of the sentence structure in the poem may be a little confusing to students, so check for comprehension before you start the discussion.

Take a deeper look:

1. The details that show what Hiawatha learns from the birds are found in lines two through five. Simply put, Hiawatha learns the birds' languages, names, and secrets, including how they build their nests and where they hide in winter.

2. The details that show what Hiawatha learns from the beasts are found in lines eight through 13. In other words, Hiawatha learns the beasts' languages, names, and secrets, including how beavers build lodges, where squirrels hide their food, how reindeer run so quickly, and why rabbits are so shy. Without the details in both stanzas, the poem would lack interest and precision of expression. If the poet had simply said that Hiawatha learns a lot about the birds and beasts, the reader would only be able to guess what he learns. The poem would lose its power to create an exact experience for the reader. It might look something like this:

Then the little Hiawatha
Learned a lot about the birds.
Then he learned about the beasts:
Beavers, squirrels, deer, and rabbits.

Not very interesting! You might want to compare the two versions and have students discuss the differences in what they understand about Hiawatha because of the detail.

Now you try it:

You might need to do this activity as a shared writing before students can do it independently. If students don't have a pet, they can imagine a wild animal or an animal they see in their neighborhood, like a crow or pigeon. Of course poems will vary a lot, but they might look something like this:

From a cat I learned its secrets,
How he hid behind my dresser,
Where he went when it was raining,
Why he purred when it was morning.

Don't worry about the rhythm or any rhyme. Just let students have fun with this. If they need additional support, let them work with a partner. When students are done writing their poems, they can highlight where they think detail makes their poem "dazzle" the most.

Dazzling Detail

Student Lesson 7

Consider the text:

Once a major crime has been discovered, the scene is soon filled with people dressed in white suits and masks. Each of these forensics experts has a special job to do. Some of the experts take photos or videos to record the crime scene exactly as they found it. Others collect evidence. This could range from clothing to fingerprints, blood, scraps of paper and fabric, and even tiny fibers on the floor or walls.

Ross Piper, *Fingerprint Wizards: The Secrets of Forensic Science*

Take a deeper look:

1. Draw a picture of the crime scene described in this paragraph.

2. What is the main idea of this paragraph? How do the details in this paragraph help you fully understand the main idea? Remember that sometimes the main idea is not the first sentence in the paragraph.

Now you try it:

Below are two sentences that start a paragraph. The first sentence sets the scene, and the second sentence gives the main idea of the paragraph. Finish this paragraph with lots of details that help the reader picture what is happening. Use Piper's paragraph as a model.

The cafeteria was full of students. Each student was doing something mysterious.

Dazzling Detail

Student Lesson 7

Commentary and Suggestions for Teachers

Lesson Objective: to understand how details focus the reader's attention and help the reader comprehend text

Consider the text:

Explain that forensic science is the use of science to solve crimes. Students may be familiar with TV shows, such as ***Bones*** or ***Sherlock***, in which characters use forensic science to solve crimes. If so, they may want to share a few ideas about forensic science. This passage contains details about the jobs of different forensic scientists. The details in this passage make it come alive for the readers.

Take a deeper look:

1. Students' pictures should reflect the details in the paragraph: people using cameras and people collecting evidence, such as fingerprints, clothing, or scraps of paper and fabric. The scientists should be dressed in white suits and masks.

2. The main idea, found in the second sentence of this paragraph, states that each of the forensics experts has a special job to do. The details focus on what the forensics experts **do** (take pictures, get fingerprints, collect physical evidence), not that they fill the scene or what they wear. Examining details helps the reader fully understand the purpose and focus of a paragraph.

Now you try it:

Students' paragraphs should focus on the mysterious things students in the cafeteria are doing. You may have to brainstorm ideas as a class before students begin writing. The more details students provide, the more clearly readers will understand what is happening in the cafeteria.

Students love detective stories and mysteries. In would be interesting to point out that readers and authors are also detectives. Readers use details to figure out information, and authors use details to give precise information. If detectives are not persistent in getting the clues they need, they will not solve the crime. If authors are not persistent in adding detail, readers will not understand the message of their writing. It would be fun to have a class discussion about readers and authors as detectives. Encourage students to be detectives and help their readers solve the mysteries.

Dazzling Detail

Student Lesson 8

Consider the text:

In only a few moments, the atmosphere changed from weary boredom to frantic hard work as Fitzy's Circus set about pitching its show tent. The rain was still coming down in torrents, threatening to turn the field into a muddy swamp. First the canvas and poles had to be unpacked, then the rigging and the stakes, along with the mallets to drive them in. Meanwhile, enclosures had to be set up for the animals, who all needed to be fed and watered after their journey.

Vicki Lockwood, *The Magnificent Lizzie Brown and the Devil's Hound*

Take a deeper look:

1. What is the main idea of this paragraph? List the details that make the main idea come alive.

2. How does the detail about the rain help you understand just how hard the work was?

Now you try it:

Finish the paragraph below with lots of specific detail. Write at least three additional sentences.

At exactly 10:05, the students changed from polite, serious scholars to wild animals as they made their way to the playground.

Dazzling Detail

Student Lesson 8

Commentary and Suggestions for Teachers

Lesson Objective: to understand how details make the writing come alive for the reader

Consider the text:

This paragraph from a novel is about setting up for a circus performance. There may be some words in the passage that some students need help to understand: "frantic" (wild), "pitching" a tent (putting up the tent and securing it to the ground), "torrents" (heavy downpour), "canvas" (the heavy fabric that the tent is made of), "rigging" (ropes that hold the tent up), "mallets" (hammers), and "enclosures" (land surrounded by fencing). Go over the vocabulary, and then have students read the passage several times. Knowing the vocabulary will help them see the importance of the detail.

Take a deeper look:

1. The main idea of the paragraph is in the first sentence: "In only a few moments, the atmosphere changed from weary boredom to frantic hard work as Fitzy's Circus set about pitching its show tent." Students should list the following details:

- "the rain was still coming down in torrents, threatening to turn the field into a muddy swamp"
- "the canvas and poles had to be unpacked"
- "the rigging and the stakes, along with the mallets to drive them in [had to be unpacked]"
- "enclosures had to be set up for the animals"

The detail is what enables students to fully understand the main idea.

2. The rain intensifies the experience for the reader. The job would be hard enough in dry weather, but it is even more difficult in the rain. And it is not just a light rain. The rain comes "down in torrents," having the potential "to turn the field into a muddy swamp." The rain will make it hard to see, and the mud will make it harder to put the tent up and take care of the animals.

Now you try it:

Students will finish the paragraph in many different ways. What is important is that they use lots of specific detail. The paragraphs should be lively and contain so much detail that any reader would know exactly what students do and look like as they leave the classroom and go to the playground.

Have students volunteer to share their finished paragraphs with the class. Then ask all students to reflect on what they have written and highlight or underline phrases that they like the most because of their use of detail.

Dazzling Detail

Student Lesson 9

Consider the text:

Their surroundings were such as to delight the heart of a couple of care-free children. The forest was filled with oaks, beeches, walnuts and sugar-maple trees, growing close together and free from underbrush. Now and then there was an open glade called a prairie or "lick," where the wild animals came to drink .... Game was plentiful—deer, bears, pheasants, wild turkeys, ducks and birds of all kinds. This, with Tom Lincoln's passion for hunting, promised good things for the family to eat, as well as bearskin rugs for the bare earth floor, and deerskin curtains for the still open door and window.

Wayne Whipple, *The Story of Young Abraham Lincoln*

Take a deeper look:

1. This paragraph describes the area around Abraham Lincoln's childhood home. Read the passage several times, and then put it away. What details do you remember about the passage? Why do you think you remember those details?

2. The author makes several general statements and then supports these general statements with specific detail. Complete the following chart to show the importance of the specific detail. You can work with a partner.

General Statement	Specific Detail That Supports the Statement	Why the Detail Is Important
Their surroundings were such as to delight the heart of a couple of care-free children.		
Game was plentiful		
This, with Tom Lincoln's passion for hunting, promised good things for the family ….		

Now you try it:

Think about your favorite place and how to describe it. Write three to five sentences describing your favorite place. Include at least two general statements that are supported by specific detail.

Dazzling Detail

Student Lesson 9

Commentary and Suggestions for Teachers

<u>Lesson Objective:</u> to understand how details provide focus and support the main idea

Consider the text:

Students should be reminded that Abraham Lincoln, the sixteenth President of the United States, lived a long time ago (1809–1865) and that life was very different then. Some words probably need clarification. "Care-free" is an old spelling of "carefree." A "glade" is a clearing in the forest. "Game" refers to animals that are hunted. Tom Lincoln was Abraham Lincoln's father. Have students read the passage several times, noting the specific detail.

Take a deeper look:

1. Students will remember different details. The important point to make here is why they remember the details. What makes the details interesting? What makes the details stand out? It will be interesting to hear the different points of view students have.

2. Charts should look something like this:

General Statement	Specific Detail That Supports the Statement	Why the Detail Is Important
"Their surroundings were such as to delight the heart of a couple of care-free children."	• the forest, filled with different kinds of trees • no underbrush • the open glade with lots of wild animals • the results of hunting (food, rugs, and curtains)	The detail makes the general statement come alive. It's not just a forest. It is a forest of specific trees we can picture in our minds. The lack of underbrush helps us see an open forest floor where children can play. And the open glade provides animal viewing and excellent hunting, necessary for sustenance and comfort.
"Game was plentiful"	specific animals: "deer, bears, pheasants, wild turkeys, ducks and birds of all kinds"	We can picture these animals. If the author had just used the word "game" without the detail, we would have an incomplete picture of the game.
"This, with Tom Lincoln's passion for hunting, promised good things for the family …"	results of the hunting: "good things for the family to eat, as well as bearskin rugs for the bare earth floor, and deerskin curtains for the still open door and window"	This is not sport hunting. The good things for the family include food, rugs, and window and door coverings. These details help the reader understand how important the hunting was and why it is connected to other things that "delight the heart."

Now you try it:

It would be helpful for students to talk about their favorite place first and then write their paragraphs. After they write, they can exchange their paragraphs with a partner. The partner should circle the general statements and underline the specific detail. The partners can then talk about how to fill the paragraph with more specific detail.

Dazzling Detail

Student Lesson 10

Consider the text:

I shall never forget the first train that ran by, I was feeding quietly near the pales which separated the meadow from the railway, when I heard a strange sound at a distance, and before I knew whence it came—with a rush and a clatter, and a puffing out of smoke—a long black train of something flew by, and was gone almost before I could draw my breath. I turned and galloped to the further side of the meadow as fast as I could go, and there I stood snorting with astonishment and fear.

Anna Sewell, *Black Beauty*

Take a deeper look:

1. ***Black Beauty*** tells the story of a horse's life, starting with his pleasant life on an English farm, continuing with his difficulties and suffering as a workhorse in London, and ending with his return to a peaceful life in the country. The narrator of the story is the horse, Black Beauty. Which period of Black Beauty's life is this passage taken from? Which details help you understand that?

2. Which details make the train sound frightening?

Now you try it:

Think about something that frightens you. Here are some suggestions of things that people are often afraid of: lightning and thunder; very dark places; certain animals such as mice, roaches, spiders, or snakes; performing in front of a large audience. Now write a paragraph that captures your fear. Use lots of specific detail so that your reader understands exactly what makes you afraid.

Dazzling Detail

Student Lesson 10

Commentary and Suggestions for Teachers

Lesson Objective: to understand the connection between author's attitude and detail

Consider the text:

Black Beauty was written in 1877, so some of the language of this passage may be a little challenging, and students may need some support before you (or they) read the passage. "Pales" are posts or rails in a fence. "Whence it came" means "where it came from." Today we generally say "catch my breath" instead of "draw my breath," but they mean the same thing. Although some of the language is old fashioned, this enduring story still has the power to capture students' imaginations. Several students may want to read the whole novel. The story is told by the horse named Black Beauty (first-person point of view), which makes the reader closely identify with the trials and triumphs of the horse. Read the passage several times and have students try to "see" the train in their minds as you read.

Take a deeper look:

1. This passage is taken from Black Beauty's early life on the farm. Details that support this are discussed in the chart below.

Detail	How it supports describing Black Beauty's early life
"the first train that ran by"	It is the <u>first</u> train. Since Black Beauty later lives in London, it is unlikely that he sees his first train later in life.
"I was feeding quietly"	Although this could also be in his last stage (back in the country), the quiet peacefulness of the detail suggests his early life on the farm.
"the meadow"	This detail could also suggest a return to the country, but it works with the other details to support the reader's understanding of Black Beauty's early life.
"I turned and galloped"	This is the action of a young horse. By the time Black Beauty returns to the country at the end of the book, he is far less likely to gallop.
"I stood snorting with astonishment and fear"	The fear Black Beauty feels is because of the newness of the train. This detail supports this passage being from Black Beauty's early life.

2. The details that make the train sound frightening include "a strange sound," "with a rush and a clatter, and a puffing out of smoke," and "a long black train [here, meaning a general sequence or order] of something flew by." The details reinforce the suddenness, noise, and strangeness of the train.

Now you try it:

Students should write about their fear using as much detail as possible. If there is time, give them an opportunity to share their paragraphs and have others in the class tell which details gave them the clearest idea of what the fear is like.

Dazzling Detail

Student Lesson 11

Consider the text:

Slavery was a nightmarish experience for black people. Captured Africans were packed like cargo in the holds of ships. The journey across the Atlantic could last as long as four months. Those who survived the trip were herded like animals to markets. Plantation owners bid high prices for the strongest and healthiest. Many buyers and sellers did not care if slave families were separated. Slaves who tried to run away or fight back were beaten, chained, or caged. Many slave traders became rich capturing people in Africa and selling them in America.

Michael Capek, *The Battle over Slavery: Causes and Effects of the U.S. Civil War*

Take a deeper look:

1. What is the main idea or topic sentence of this paragraph? List the details that support the main idea.

2. Read the last sentence of the paragraph again. Does this sentence contain detail that directly supports the main idea? Why do you think the author included the last sentence in this paragraph?

Now you try it:

Think about the benefits of freedom for all people. Write a topic sentence that clearly states how important freedom is for all people. Now list all of the details you can think of to support the topic sentence and make the paragraph come alive. Share your list with a partner. Add new ideas to your list. Write the paragraph (at least four sentences) using enough detail to help your reader understand exactly how important freedom is for all people.

Dazzling Detail

Student Lesson 11

Commentary and Suggestions for Teachers

Lesson Objective: to understand how details support the main idea and convey the author's attitude

Consider the text:

Nonfiction text needs lots of detail too. Without detail, the reader cannot get a clear and accurate understanding of the information. Have students read the passage several times. Ask them to write down any words or ideas they do not understand and, if needed, help them fully comprehend the passage.

Take a deeper look:

1. The main idea of the passage is stated in the first sentence: "Slavery was a nightmarish experience for black people." Here are the details that support the main idea:

- "Captured Africans were packed like cargo in the holds of ships."
- "The journey across the Atlantic could last as long as four months."
- "Those who survived the trip were herded like animals to markets."
- "Many buyers and sellers did not care if slave families were separated."
- "Slaves who tried to run away or fight back were beaten, chained, or caged."

I would not include the sentences about high prices or the last sentence because they do not directly support the main idea.

2. The last sentence of the paragraph does not contain detail that directly supports the main idea. The fact that many slave traders became rich does not help readers understand why slavery was a nightmarish experience. However, the last sentence does reinforce the horror of slavery by contrasting the lives of slave traders with the lives of the slaves.

Now you try it:

Once students have their lists, have them share with a partner or in a small group. The exchange of ideas is an essential part of the writing process. Students should add new ideas to their lists and then write the paragraph. The aim is to let their readers know exactly why freedom is important for all people.

Dazzling Detail

Student Lesson 12

Consider the text:

"Listen, man-cub," said the Bear, and his voice rumbled like thunder on a hot night. "I have taught thee all the Law of the Jungle for all the peoples of the jungle—except the Monkey-Folk who live in the trees. They have no law …. They have no speech of their own, but use the stolen words which they overhear when they listen, and peep, and wait up above in branches. Their way is not our way. They are without leaders. They have no remembrance. They boast and chatter and pretend that they are a great people about to do great affairs in the jungle, but the falling of a nut turns their minds to laughter and all is forgotten."

Rudyard Kipling, The Jungle Book

Take a deeper look:

1. The story this passage is taken from is about a boy named Mowgli, who is raised by wolves in the jungle of India. The animals become his teachers. One of his teachers is the Bear. Here the Bear is contrasting all of the "peoples of the jungle" with the monkeys. What does the Bear think about the "Monkey-Folk"? In other words, what is the main idea of this paragraph?

2. List the details that support the main idea about the "Monkey-Folk." How do the details help you understand what it means to be without law?

Now you try it:

Think about a food you do not like. Write a paragraph explaining what you don't like about the food. Start with a clear topic sentence and add at least three sentences with details that support the topic sentence. Be certain your attitude toward the food is very clear.

Dazzling Detail

Student Lesson 12

Commentary and Suggestions for Teachers

<u>Lesson Objective:</u> to understand how details build understanding of the main idea or focus of the text

Consider the text:

Students may be familiar with this story. They may have read the book or watched the Disney movie. The Bear (Baloo) helps save Mowgli when the monkeys capture him. The monkeys are cast as wild and irresponsible, in contrast to the other animals of the jungle. Have students read the passage and think carefully about what the main idea is.

Take a deeper look:

1. The main idea of this paragraph is that the monkeys have no law. The implication of this (drawn by contrasting the monkeys with "all the peoples of the jungle" who obey the "Law of the Jungle") is that the monkeys are uncivilized, without history, order, intelligence, or understanding. The Bear finds the monkeys and their behavior disgraceful.

2. The details that support the main idea are

   - "They have no speech of their own, but use the stolen words which they overhear when they listen, and peep, and wait up above in branches."
   - "Their way is not our way."
   - "They are without leaders."
   - "They have no remembrance."
   - "They boast and chatter and pretend that they are a great people about to do great affairs in the jungle, but the falling of a nut turns their minds to laughter and all is forgotten."

Without the detail it would not be clear why the Bear thinks it is so bad to have no law. Law here is equated with order, civilization, leadership, history, and meaning. The other "peoples of the jungle" have speech of their own, have leaders, have history, and follow through with what they intend to do. The details set up the contrast between the monkeys and the rest of the jungle animals and make it clear that the monkeys fail to measure up because they have no law.

Now you try it:

Have students write their topic sentence and list details that support the topic sentence. They can then write their paragraph and share it with the class. It would be fun to chart out the different foods students pick and why they don't like the food. Then the class can complete a shared writing of the class's least favorite foods, with a clear topic sentence, sharp focus, unquestionable attitude, and specific supporting details.

Additional Resources for Dazzling Detail

Dazzling Detail Chart

Topic	Main Idea (Focus)	Supporting Details	How the Details Help You Understand the Main Idea

Examples and Nonexamples

Below are samples of text students can examine to help them understand the importance of using concrete detail in their writing. These examples and nonexamples allow students to

- experience how details help the reader identify what is important,
- compare the different levels of detail using evidence to explain which example is the best, and
- look at their own writing and see what they need to do to make the writing come alive.

Have students read all three examples and then use the chart to rank the passages' use of detail and explain why detail is essential to quality writing.

Cheese Pizza by N. Danaher

Ex. 1: Cheese pizza is the best kind of pizza. It tastes really good and I like it.

Ex. 2: Where would I be without cheese pizza? Some say it is plain, but I say simplicity is a form of art. The first bite tells me that this pizza is meant for me. I bite down and see the salty, yet sweet, red tomato sauce bulge out of the blanket of cheese like hot lava. I pull the slice away from my mouth, but the cheese fights to stay connected. Finally, I tear it away with my teeth. The crust is so buttery and crisp that I stop and think, "With all that's happening in my mouth, who needs toppings?"

Ex. 3: Cheese pizza is the best kind of pizza. The crust is crunchy, the sauce is warm, and the cheese is gooey.

Abstract	Some Detail	Alive with Detail
Example number:	Example number:	Example number:
Why it doesn't work:	Why it's better but still not great:	Why it's the best:

Thunderstorms at Night by N. Danaher

Ex. 1: Nighttime thunderstorms are loud and keep me awake. The lightning is too bright, the thunder is too loud, and the rain sprays hard against my window.

Ex. 2: Thunderstorms are scary, especially when they come at night.

Ex. 3: Without warning, a flash of light enters my bedroom and I'm awake. Another one follows in its footsteps. After that, I hear a slow and long rumble and I know a thunderstorm is approaching. Within five minutes, thunder and lightning are competing like they are on some talent show, and now rain wants a turn. Flash! Boom! Splash! Will it ever end? I need my sleep!

Abstract	Some Detail	Alive with Detail
Example number:	Example number:	Example number:
Why it doesn't work:	Why it's better but still not great:	Why it's the best:

Irresistible Imagery

Introduction

Imagery is the use of words to recreate a sensory experience. People often think imagery refers to creating a visual picture for the reader, but imagery includes any experience of the five senses. In other words, imagery captures in words what we **see**, what we **hear**, what we **touch**, what we **smell**, and what we **taste**. Visual imagery is most common, but authors experiment with all of the senses in their writing. Imagery is another way to make writing alive and interesting.

It is difficult to separate imagery from diction and detail. In fact, imagery depends on precise word choice and specific detail. The difference lies only in the author's focus: Imagery uses words and details to capture a sensory experience. For example, if we take a passage like this, "There was a furious storm in the forest. Lightning illuminated the tops of the trees and thunder exploded. The earth trembled and the air smelled of burning wood," we see precise word choice, specific detail, and imagery. The words and details create the imagery, appealing to sight, touch, sound, and smell. Effective imagery is built on effective diction and detail but draws the reader's attention specifically to the senses. It is another way to connect the reader to the text. The more specific the imagery is, the more powerful it is as a tool for the author.

Students can learn how imagery helps them comprehend complex text. They can learn to identify different types of images and to understand how imagery contributes to an understanding of a text. They can also become better authors themselves by experimenting with imagery, creating a specific experience for their readers. But it takes practice. That's what this chapter is about. These lessons will provide students with the tools they need in order to understand the effect imagery has on reading comprehension. The lessons will also help them to make good decisions about using images in their own writing.

The lessons are designed to progress in difficulty in terms of both the text students analyze and the activities students participate in. However, it is certainly not necessary to use every lesson or to go in a particular order. In addition, each lesson's commentary and suggestions for teachers are exactly that: suggestions that you may or may not use in your work with students. You are the experts. You know your kids. Our intent is only to provide support for very busy professionals.

Of note are some threads that run through all of the Irresistible Imagery lessons. First, it is important that students be able to see the passages that form the foundation of each lesson. You can run off individual copies of the passages. Alternatively, you can print them on chart paper or a whiteboard or project them. Another thread is the Irresistible Imagery Chart. Students can use this chart to collect images they find particularly appealing. There is a blank chart you can use at the end of this chapter on page 101. Finally, we have included additional practice with examples and nonexamples of how irresistible imagery improves writing. This practice can be found on pages 102–103.

We hope these lessons are engaging and helpful for you and your students. With practice, students can learn the power of irresistible imagery and go a long way toward finding their own voices.

Irresistible Imagery

Warm-up Lessons

The warm-up lessons are designed to introduce students to each element of voice. These lessons use simple text written to illustrate the specific element of voice under consideration—here, imagery. The questions direct students' attention to the purpose and power of understanding imagery in reading and using imagery in writing. In addition, we provide a brief review of the importance of imagery and suggest relevant academic language to include on word walls and in conversations with students.

Why imagery is important:
- Imagery helps the reader connect to text through the five senses.
- Imagery uses precise words and specific details.
- Imagery makes writing alive and interesting.
- Imagery helps with reading comprehension.

Warm-up 1

I watched the river twist and turn,

The water white with foam.

I saw some moss and dark green fern

And found a rabbit's home.

> N. Dean

1. What kind of imagery is used in this poem? (visual and implied river sounds)

2. What effect does the imagery have on the reader's understanding of the poem? (The imagery allows the reader to experience the scene described in the poem as the author intends. The river is not a peaceful, deep river. It twists and turns and has rough water. But the riverbank is peaceful: The ground is covered with moss and dark green fern, green being a peaceful color. The "home" belongs to a rabbit, a gentle animal, contributing to the peace and quiet of the riverbank.)

Warm-up 2

Blood is not just the stuff that leaks out of your newly scraped knee. Blood's main purpose is to make sure that every part of your body stays healthy and strong. Blood carries the oxygen and nutrients that each part of your body needs to work correctly. Blood also keeps us warm, cools us off, and fights infection.

T.W. Dean

1. What kind of imagery is used in this passage? (The imagery appeals to our senses of sight and touch. The first sentence lets the reader "feel" and "see" an uncomfortable scrape. We can picture blood carrying nutrients and oxygen to parts of the body. We also get a sense of blood's importance by association with being warm in cold weather and cool in the heat.)

2. Why is the imagery important? (The imagery here supports the main idea—that blood's main purpose is to make sure that every part of your body stays healthy and strong.)

Word Wall Suggestions

evidence, image, sensory experience, five senses: sight, sound, touch, smell, taste

Irresistible Imagery

Student Lesson 1

Consider the text:

A banana spider is big and hairy. Banana spiders have 8 legs.
Banana spiders have 8 eyes. Banana spiders are long spiders ....
A banana spider has big red fangs. It has long hairy legs.

Anne Giulieri, ***The Banana Spider***

Take a deeper look:

1. Imagery helps us explore the world. Imagery helps us see, hear, touch, smell, or taste the things the author describes. Can you see the spider in your mind? Can you hear it or smell it? Do you have some idea of what it feels like? Do you know what a banana spider tastes like from these images?

2. Draw a picture of a banana spider. How do the words help you draw the spider?

Now you try it:

Work with a partner. Listen to your partner describe a pet or an animal he or she has seen at the zoo or in his/her neighborhood. Try to draw the animal as your partner has described it. What images help you? Now let your partner listen to you as you describe an animal. Can your partner draw the animal? What images helped him or her?

Irresistible Imagery

Student Lesson 1

Commentary and Suggestions for Teachers

Lesson Objective: to use sight imagery to demonstrate understanding of text

Consider the text:

Explain that banana spiders like to hide in banana leaves, which is why they are called banana spiders. Have students talk about the kinds of spiders they have seen and how big they are. Prepare students to listen to the passage by being quiet and closing their eyes. Then ask them to picture the banana spider as you read the words aloud. Have them share some ideas.

Take a deeper look:

1. The imagery in this passage is primarily visual (sight imagery). We know the spider is big (for a spider!) and hairy, with eight eyes and red fangs. When we read these sentences, we cannot hear, smell, or taste the spider. We do, however, have some idea of what the spider feels like: It is hairy. Ask students to think of other things that are hairy. You could also bring in examples of hairy things for them to touch and describe. If students say they can hear, smell, or taste the spider, read the passage again and ask them for their evidence. This is a good time to introduce the importance of evidence. When we read, we can't say the passage means whatever we want it to. We have to base our understanding on what the passage actually says.

2. The pictures should be based on the passage. The spider should have eight long, hairy legs; eight eyes; and red fangs. Talk about the pictures and how they relate to the words. Display the passage and circle the words that help students see the spider. Begin a class Irresistible Imagery Chart (page 101), noting words that help us see, hear, touch, smell, or taste something.

Now you try it:

This activity will run more smoothly if you have students choose an animal and brainstorm ideas about the way it looks for homework. Students will use their time more productively if they come in ready with ideas for their partner.

The more specific the images are, the better the pictures will be. Students should consider size, shape, and color. They can also describe specific features like teeth, eyes, ears, tails, and the like. The goal is that their partner can "see" the animal from the specific images. If students want to make up an animal, that is fine. They just have to use specific visual images to describe their imaginary animal.

Irresistible Imagery

Student Lesson 2

Consider the text:

> Little Clara May was very, very small.
>
> But what was most extraordinary was her hair was really tall!
>
> She didn't need a pencil case, a schoolbag, or lunch box,
>
> Instead she stored her gear in her big, strong, curly locks!

Helen Poole, ***Clara's Crazy Curls***

Take a deeper look:

1. What does Clara May look like? How do you know?

2. Think about the imagery in this passage. What words help you "see" Clara May's hair? What do you think Clara May stores in her hair? Name three things Clara May might store in her hair.

Now you try it:

Draw a picture of someone with crazy hair. What are some words you could use to help others picture this crazy hair? Share your words with your class.

Irresistible Imagery

Student Lesson 2

Commentary and Suggestions for Teachers

Lesson Objective: to use precise words and specific details to create a clear visual image

Consider the text:

Read the passage several times, and make certain students understand all of the words. They may have trouble with "gear" (the stuff students take to school) and "locks" (pieces of hair). This passage contains visual imagery.

Take a deeper look:

1. Clara May is very small and has very tall, curly hair. We find that out in lines one, two, and four, which clearly describe her. Students could also picture Clara May with all kinds of school gear in her hair, suggested in lines three and four.

2. The words that help students "see" Clara May's hair are "her hair was really tall" and "her big, strong, curly locks." This is visual imagery that enables students to fully participate in the scene. Clara May can store anything that usually fits in a pencil box, schoolbag, or lunch box in her hair. This might include pencils, markers, scissors, books, paper, a sandwich, a drink, fruit, and the like. Students should have fun thinking about all of the things Clara May could have in her hair.

Now you try it:

Answers will vary. The important part of this activity is to help students create a visual image with words. Let them talk about crazy hair first and then draw their pictures. Add a selection of words that create a clear visual image to your class Irresistible Imagery Chart.

Irresistible Imagery

Student Lesson 3

Consider the text:

On the frontier, pioneer families continued to struggle. Great Plains settlers worried about prairie fires, tornadoes, and dust storms that filled the air with brown grit. During winter wild blizzards covered their small homes with snow and ice. Settlers strung ropes from the house to the barn, so no one would be lost in a blizzard.

Heather E. Schwartz, ***The Foul, Filthy American Frontier: The Disgusting Details About the Journey Out West***

Take a deeper look:

1. Which image in the passage tells you what dust storms feel and look like?

2. What do the words "wild blizzards" make you see in your mind? How did the settlers keep from getting lost in such a blizzard? Discuss your answers with a partner. Be sure to look for images in the passage that provide evidence for your answers.

Now you try it:

Work with a partner to write some visual images. Look at the list below. Work together to think of and write visual images to describe each thing in the list. Your images should help others "see" what you are writing about. Share your images with another group.

- A hot summer day
- A playground
- A classroom at the end of a day

Irresistible Imagery

Student Lesson 3

Commentary and Suggestions for Teachers

<u>Lesson Objective</u>: to understand how images connect the reader to text and to make writing alive and interesting through imagery

Consider the text:

This book is about the families that settled the American frontier between 1844 and 1866. The book focuses on the difficulties and hardships these settlers faced. This passage describes the difficulties settlers had with the severe weather on the Great Plains. Students may need help with a few vocabulary words: "grit" (sand and small pieces of stone) and "blizzard" (a big, windy snowstorm). If students are unfamiliar with the settling of the American West, it would be helpful to give them some background information. There are many student-friendly sites on the Internet describing this period of American history.

Take a deeper look:

1. The image that helps readers "see" and "feel" the dust storms is "dust storms that filled the air with brown grit." The air is "filled" with sand and dirt, making it hard to see anything but the brown air. And it is "grit," not just dust. It is harsh on the skin and gets in eyes and ears. The imagery in this sentence helps students see and feel what the settlers saw and felt. It would be helpful to bring in something gritty that students could feel. It will help them understand the image in the passage.

2. These are not just blizzards. They are "wild blizzards." The words should help students "see" lots of snow on the ground, wind blowing snow everywhere, and houses covered with snow and ice. The last sentence in the passage provides a visual image of how the settlers traveled from the house to the barn without getting lost in the blizzard: They "strung ropes from the house to the barn" so that they could hold onto the rope to get from one place to another. This image reinforces the wildness of the blizzard, snow and wind so fierce that the settlers could not even see. As students discuss these images, be certain they gather evidence from the text. It is easy to imagine the roofs blowing off the houses, but there is no evidence for that in the text. Help students to see the importance of gathering evidence from the text to answer questions rather than writing a new or supplementary passage from their imaginations.

Now you try it:

Students should come up with a variety of images. Give them time to work with a partner and then share their work. If they are stuck, here are some suggestions to get them started:

- A hot summer day: The pavement was so hot that steam floated up to the treetops. Sweat covered me from head to toe, dripping off my nose.
- A playground: The slide reflected the sunshine and clouds. The kids on the swings pumped their legs and went higher and higher.
- A classroom at the end of a day: The students gathered their books, lunch boxes, and papers. Many students looked at the door and tapped their feet, waiting to go home.

Irresistible Imagery

Student Lesson 4

Consider the text:

A low, menacing growl came from behind them.

There was another growl, much louder now, and the snoring stopped.

"Oh no," Cecilia said.

A shape uncurled itself from the long grass in front of them. Two dots glowed. Two huge eyes. Another lion. A huge lion. They had almost walked right on top of it. Silver moonlight stained its coarse fur as it got slowly to its feet.

Brian Falkner, *Northwood*

Take a deeper look:

1. What do you "see" when you read this passage?

2. What do you "hear" when you read this passage?

Now you try it:

When you go to the cafeteria, listen carefully to the sounds you hear. Think of each distinct sound and, if possible, write down your observations. When you are back in the classroom, talk about these sounds with a partner. With your partner, write a description about two of these sounds. Use strong images so that others can "hear" these sounds just as you do.

Irresistible Imagery

Student Lesson 4

Commentary and Suggestions for Teachers

Lesson Objective: to understand how imagery shapes the reader's comprehension and to recreate sounds with written imagery

Consider the text:

This passage is from a story about a girl who rescues a dog but winds up in a dark forest filled with lions. Her adventures show the importance of kindness, understanding, and cleverness. This passage is filled with both visual and auditory imagery. Read the passage several times aloud to give students a feeling for how imagery contributes to the reader's understanding of the passage. Students may need to know that "menacing" means "scary."

Take a deeper look:

1. Visual images include the lion's "shape uncurl[ing] itself from the long grass," the two glowing dots (eyes), the huge lion, and the "silver moonlight stain[ing] its coarse fur as it got slowly to its feet." The visual images help the reader fully participate in the scene.

2. The sounds in the passage are the sounds of the lions. Notice that the lion's growl is not just a growl. It's "a low, menacing growl." The auditory image is specific and clear. There is a louder growl, then the lions stop snoring, and there is silence, which almost seems like the loudest and most menacing sound of all. The auditory imagery, like the visual imagery, brings the reader into the scene and helps him or her fully understand what is happening.

Now you try it:

It would be helpful to prepare students for this activity right before they go to the cafeteria. You can prompt them to pay attention to the sounds they hear and even write down descriptions of the sounds in a notebook that they bring with them.

Students' images will vary, but be certain that they are using specific images, not abstract description. For example, instead of saying "the cafeteria was noisy," they might say, "Three students dropped their trays. Everyone screamed when they heard a loud crash." What is important is that students work on specific, vivid imagery.

Irresistible Imagery

Student Lesson 5

Consider the text:

When the girl returned, some hours later, she carried a tray, with a cup
of fragrant tea steaming on it; and a plate piled up with very hot buttered
toast, cut thick, very brown on both sides, with the butter running through
the holes in it in great golden drops, like honey from the honeycomb. The
smell of that buttered toast simply talked to Toad, and with no uncertain
voice; talked of warm kitchens, of breakfasts on bright frosty mornings,
of cosy parlour firesides on winter evenings, when one's ramble was over
and slippered feet were propped on the fender; of the purring of contented
cats, and the twitter of sleepy canaries.

Kenneth Grahame, *The Wind in the Willows*

Take a deeper look:

1. Read the passage several times. Remember that imagery is the creation of
sensory experiences in writing and that the five senses are sight, smell, sound,
touch, and taste. List the images from the passage that appeal to each of the five
senses. Your list can be in chart form like this:

Sight	Sound	Smell	Touch	Taste

2. What would the passage be like without the imagery? Try to write the passage
without any images.

Now you try it:

Write three sentences that describe a time you ate your favorite meal. The first
sentence should appeal to the sense of sight. The second sentence should appeal
to the sense of smell, and the third sentence should appeal to the sense of taste. Try
to write so that your reader completely understands what you liked about the meal.

Irresistible Imagery

Student Lesson 5

Commentary and Suggestions for Teachers

Lesson Objective: to create an experience for the reader using the five senses

Consider the text:

This passage creates a scene and brings the reader into the experience through imagery. Read the passage (or have students read it) several times to get the full impact of the imagery. There are a few words that you may need to clarify for students for deep understanding. "Cosy" and "parlour" are British spellings of the words "cozy" and "parlor." A "ramble" is a walk or stroll, and a "fender" is the guard in front of a fireplace. Toad is a character in the story.

Take a deeper look:

1. This passage is full of all sorts of imagery. Although placement may vary, charts should look something like this:

Sight	Sound	Smell	Touch	Taste
• "she carried a tray" • "steaming" • "a plate piled up" • "toast, cut thick, very brown on both sides" • "butter running through the holes in it in great golden drops" • "breakfasts on bright frosty mornings" • "slippered feet were propped on the fender"	• "smell of that buttered toast simply talked to Toad" • "talked of warm kitchens" • "the purring of contented cats" • "the twitter of sleepy canaries"	• "a cup of fragrant tea" • "smell of that buttered toast"	• "very hot buttered toast" • "warm kitchens" • "cosy parlour firesides on winter evenings"	• "the butter running through the holes in it in great golden drops, like honey from the honeycomb" • "breakfasts on bright frosty mornings"

2. Without the imagery, the passage would be dull and pointless. The imagery allows the reader to experience the scene as if he or she were there. Without the imagery, the passage might sound something like this: **"The girl brought some tea and toast. Toad liked the things that she brought."** It's pretty boring!

Now you try it:

Sentences will vary but should appeal to the senses of sight, smell, and taste. If students can include all five senses, so much the better! Have students share their sentences.

Irresistible Imagery

Student Lesson 6

Consider the text:

Outside Princeton, Washington instructed his men to build huge fires. When the British saw the fiery orange glow, they thought the Americans had set up their camp for the night. Instead, Washington moved his men to a position where they could launch a surprise attack.

Michael Burgan, ***The Untold Story of the Black Regiment: Fighting in the Revolutionary War***

Take a deeper look:

1. Which of the five senses is most useful in helping you understand what happens in this passage? Explain your answer.

2. How would the power of the passage change if it had been written like this?

"Outside Princeton, Washington instructed his men to build fires. When the British saw the fires, they thought the Americans had already camped."

Now you try it:

Read the sentences below several times. Now try to make them more powerful and interesting by adding specific images. You can add whatever you like to the sentences. Use Burgan's paragraph as a model.

Outside my house, there was a delivery truck. When I saw the truck, I thought someone had sent me a present.

Irresistible Imagery

Student Lesson 6

Commentary and Suggestions for Teachers

Lesson Objective: to understand how imagery connects the reader to the experience of the text and to write a passage using imagery to make the writing more powerful and interesting

Consider the text:

This passage is about a battle in the Revolutionary War. Authors of nonfiction use imagery in the same way that authors of fiction do: to help the reader understand exactly what the author is trying to communicate. Here, the author creates a clear image of the preparation for battle. There are no particular obstacles to comprehension in this passage.

Take a deeper look:

1. The primary sense that is used in this passage is sight. The reader can "see" several "huge fires." In addition, the British are tricked by the "fiery orange glow" of the fires, a visual image that allows the reader to understand exactly how the British see and are tricked by the fires. Students might try to make a case for the sense of touch since fire is hot, but the heat of the fire is not stressed in the passage. This would be a good time to remind students that they must gather their evidence from the passage, not their prior experience.

2. The rewritten passage is much more abstract and bland. It does not give the reader a powerful picture of what is happening. The imagery in the original passage brings the reader into the scene and helps him/her fully understand the impact of events.

Now you try it:

Sentences will vary a lot, but they should look something like this:

Outside my house, I saw a huge delivery truck. A strong-looking man stepped out of the truck carrying a round, red box. When I saw the man headed toward my house, I was certain my aunt, the one with curly hair and sparkly shoes, had sent me a present I might not like.

The more specific the imagery, the better the writing will be.

Irresistible Imagery

Student Lesson 7

Consider the text:

There was a row of trees just off the road, and as they drew closer, Lizzie saw it was the fringe of an enormous park. White stone buildings showed through the trees. The rain brought out the sad, sweet smell of cypresses.

Vicki Lockwood, *The Magnificent Lizzie Brown and the Devil's Hound*

Take a deeper look:

1. What images help you "see" the scene?

2. What does the smell imagery ("the sad, sweet smell of cypresses") add to the way you experience the scene? How can something smell sad?

Now you try it:

Think about something you think "smells" happy. Use the following sentence stem to write a sentence that contains a "smell" image that you associate with being happy.

The campfire brought out the _____
smell of _____ .

Irresistible Imagery

Student Lesson 7

Commentary and Suggestions for Teachers

Lesson Objective: to use precise words and specific details to create an experience based on smell

Consider the text:

Lizzie is the main character in this novel. In this scene, she is approaching the field where she and her friends will set up a circus that allows her to exhibit her magical powers. A few words may need clarification: "fringe" is a border or edge and "cypress" is a kind of tree with needle-like leaves. There are many different kinds of cypress trees, and images are readily available on the Internet. Even better, if you could bring in a branch from a cypress tree and let students see, touch, and smell it, it would help students understand the reference more fully.

The imagery here helps the reader understand what the scene looks and feels like. Note that there is a lot of overlap between diction and imagery. For example, the author chooses a specific word, "fringe," to describe the row of trees that surrounds the park. This carefully chosen diction evokes a visual image: the trees forming a decorative border around the park. It is a matter of focus. Diction is specific word choice. Imagery is the use of sensory experiences to create an effect. They are interdependent.

Take a deeper look:

1. The images that help the reader "see" the scene are:
   - "a row of trees just off the road,"
   - "the fringe of an enormous park," and
   - "White stone buildings showed through the trees."

The images work together to create a picture that forms the background of the action.

2. The smell imagery of the cypress trees adds a sense of mystery, foreboding, and darkness to the scene. If you crush the needles of a cypress tree with your fingers, they do smell sweet—an earthy, healthy sweetness. Rain can bring out that smell. The sadness might refer to the fact that some cypress trees lose their needles in the winter. This gives the trees a feeling of impending hardship and trouble. It foreshadows things to come in the novel. You might have to take some time to teach students about cypress trees and trees that lose their leaves in the winter.

Now you try it:

To prepare students for this activity, it would be helpful to bring in scented markers, unlit candles, peppermints, an orange, or anything that gives off a pleasant smell. Then give students an opportunity to talk about the feelings associated with those smells. After that, students can work on their sentences. Students can associate happy smells with food, holidays, people, pets, or anything else they can think of. Their sentences should look something like this:

The campfire brought out the rich, friendly smell of roasting hot dogs.

Irresistible Imagery

Student Lesson 8

Consider the text:

The way light behaves sometimes plays tricks on our eyes. When light passes through a window or water it changes speeds and can refract. Refraction means the light bends. When light changes speeds and bends, objects don't always look normal. For instance, a straw in a glass of water looks broken. We see the straw because light reflects off it and into our eyes. But the light coming from the bottom part of the straw passes through both water and glass. The two materials bend the light so much the straw looks broken.

Jody Jensen Shaffer, *Vampires and Light*

Take a deeper look:

1. Read this passage carefully. Note that this is informational text. The author is trying to teach you something—in this case, about light. To help you learn about light, the author uses visual imagery. What images help you understand what a straw in a glass of water looks like when light bends?

2. How would it change your understanding of the paragraph if we left out the images, like this?

"Light can play tricks on us. Sometimes light can make things look abnormal and can even make a straw in a glass of water look broken."

Now you try it:

Think about something you know a lot about. It could be something in science or a hobby or an activity you like doing. Start with a clear topic sentence stating your main idea (like the author did in the passage about light). Then write two or three more sentences that use imagery to help your reader understand your topic sentence. Share your paragraph with a partner or the class.

Irresistible Imagery

Student Lesson 8

Commentary and Suggestions for Teachers

Lesson Objective: to understand how imagery contributes to the reader's comprehension of informational text

Consider the text:

Students may need some help with this passage. Although the words are not difficult, students may need some background and support to understand refraction. You might want to do the experiment with a straw in a glass of water so that students can see what the passage is explaining.

Take a deeper look:

1. The images that help students understand what a straw in a glass of water looks like when light bends include:

- "light passes through a window or water,"
- "a straw in a glass of water looks broken,"
- "We see the straw because light reflects off it and into our eyes," and
- "two materials bend the light so much the straw looks broken."

2. If the author left out the images, it would be very difficult to understand the passage. What does it mean for things to look "abnormal"? Why would the straw look broken? Why is this a "trick"? We would not understand anything about refraction, why light bends, or why refracted light changes the way we see something. Imagery, like pictures, helps us understand our world.

Now you try it:

It would be very helpful for you to model the writing of a paragraph about a hobby or activity of your own before students write their paragraphs. Display your paragraph prominently so that students can see how you use imagery to support informational text. As students plan their own paragraphs, they should think about something they know well. They may want to talk about topics for a few minutes before they start writing. Their first sentence should be a specific and clear statement of the main idea. The rest of the paragraph should use imagery to support the main idea. They can use any sense experience: sight, sound, smell, touch, or taste. Students should share their completed paragraphs with a partner or the class.

Irresistible Imagery

Student Lesson 9

Consider the text:

She slept a long time, and when she awakened Mrs. Medlock had bought a lunchbasket at one of the stations and they had some chicken and cold beef and bread and butter and some hot tea. The rain seemed to be streaming down more heavily than ever and everybody in the station wore wet and glistening waterproofs. The guard lighted the lamps in the carriage, and Mrs. Medlock cheered up very much over her tea and chicken and beef. She ate a great deal and afterward fell asleep herself, and Mary sat and stared at her and watched her fine bonnet slip on one side until she herself fell asleep once more in the corner of the carriage, lulled by the splashing of the rain against the windows. It was quite dark when she awakened again. The train had stopped at a station and Mrs. Medlock was shaking her.

Frances Hodgson Burnett, ***The Secret Garden***

Take a deeper look:

1. List the images from the passage that appeal to the five senses. Be sure you have evidence from the passage to support your list. Your list can be in chart form like this:

Sight	Sound	Smell	Touch	Taste

2. Rewrite the sentence below **without** the images. How does it change your understanding of the passage?

"She ate a great deal and afterward fell asleep herself, and Mary sat and stared at her and watched her fine bonnet slip on one side until she herself fell asleep once more in the corner of the carriage, lulled by the splashing of the rain against the windows."

Now you try it:

Write a sentence about a time you rode in a car, bus, or train while it was raining. Use at least one sound image and one sight image in your sentence.

Irresistible Imagery

Student Lesson 9

Commentary and Suggestions for Teachers

Lesson Objective: to understand how imagery brings the reader into a scene or an experience

Consider the text:

In this passage from **The Secret Garden**, Mary, one of the main characters, is traveling in a carriage to her uncle's house for the first time. Mrs. Medlock is the housekeeper who accompanies Mary on the trip. A "waterproof" is a raincoat. If there are students in the class who are familiar with the story, it would be nice to have them give a short summary. If not, it would be a wonderful enrichment activity to read this treasure of a book to them.

Take a deeper look:

1. Students can call out the images in a class discussion, annotate text, or make individual or group charts. It would be helpful for students to have their own copies of the passage to highlight the evidence. They could choose a colored pencil for each sense and underline or circle the evidence. For example, if they chose yellow for touch, they would underline "Mrs. Medlock was shaking her" in yellow. This annotation method could also be used for helping students plan their own sentences. A student chart should look something like this:

Sight	Sound	Smell	Touch	Taste
• "Mrs. Medlock had bought a lunchbasket at one of the stations and they had some chicken and cold beef and bread and butter and some hot tea" • "rain seemed to be streaming down more heavily than ever" • "everybody in the station wore wet and glistening waterproofs" • "The guard lighted the lamps" • "Mary sat and stared at her and watched her fine bonnet slip on one side" • "It was quite dark"	• "lulled by the splashing of the rain against the windows"	• none	• "Mrs. Medlock was shaking her"	• "they had some chicken and cold beef and bread and butter and some hot tea" • "Mrs. Medlock cheered up very much over her tea and chicken and beef"

Students might say that the food smells good, but that is speculation. There is no textual evidence for that.

2. Without the images, the sentence might look something like this: **"Mrs. Medlock ate a lot and slept. Mary watched her and fell asleep, and it rained**." All the reader is left with is a hint of the scene. We get no glimpse into Mary's personality; and we have no insight into the atmosphere or mood of the trip without the "splashing of the rain against the windows" that "lulls" Mary to sleep.

Now you try it:

Encourage students to be creative and write sentences that bring the reader into the scene through imagery. Have students share their sentences.

Irresistible Imagery

Student Lesson 10

Consider the text:

> I remember the long, slow sigh of the sea as we raced in the sun,
> To dry ourselves after our swimming; and how we would run
> With a cry and a crash through the foam as it creamed on the shore,
> Then back to bask in the warm dry gold of the sand once more.
>
> Alfred Noyes, "Pirates," *Collected Poems*

Take a deeper look:

1. In this poem, the narrator is remembering what it was like when he was a boy at the beach, pretending to be a pirate with his friends. Close your eyes and listen as your teacher or a classmate reads the stanza several times. What images do you remember from listening to the poem? Why do you think you remember those particular images?

2. Consider the image, "we would run / With a cry and a crash through the foam as it creamed on the shore." What picture comes to your mind from the words "it creamed on the shore"?

Now you try it:

Write a four-line poem about something you remember. Start your poem with the words, "I remember …." Your poem should contain at least one visual image and one sound image. It doesn't matter if your poem rhymes or not.

Irresistible Imagery

Student Lesson 10

Commentary and Suggestions for Teachers

Lesson Objective: to make writing come alive through imagery

Consider the text:

Before you start this lesson, it would be helpful to have a discussion about memories, especially what students remember about an earlier time in childhood, a trip or vacation, or a game they played with their friends. Then have students close their eyes as you read the stanza aloud several times, emphasizing the images. You might want students to draw a picture of the scene before they begin discussing the specific images.

Take a deeper look:

1. Student responses will vary—there are many vivid images in this stanza. It will be interesting to hear why students remember specific images. Perhaps they just like the mental picture. Perhaps the image reminds them of a similar experience. This would be a good time to help students understand the importance of making personal connections to what they are reading.

2. We don't usually use the verb "cream" in this way. We "cream" ingredients in baking or "cream" an opponent in a game. This unusual use of the verb surprises us and creates a clear visual image of the foam from the waves forming a cream-like deposit on the shore. Students should describe the visual image as thick, white foam, similar to whipped cream or meringue. Note again that the elements of diction, detail, and imagery often overlap and are interdependent.

Now you try it:

Let students have fun with this activity. It doesn't matter if the poem rhymes or has a particular rhythm. The focus here should be on crafting a clear memory, filled with vivid images that make the experience come alive.

Irresistible Imagery

Student Lesson 11

Consider the text:

The animal he bestrode was a broken-down plow-horse, that had outlived almost everything but its viciousness. He was gaunt and shagged, with a ewe neck, and a head like a hammer; his rusty mane and tail were tangled and knotted with burs; one eye had lost its pupil, and was glaring and spectral, but the other had the gleam of a genuine devil in it.

Washington Irving, "The Legend of Sleepy Hollow"

Take a deeper look:

1. Draw a picture of the horse. Try to use as many of the images from the passage as you can.

2. What do you know about the horse's personality? Which image tells you the most about the horse's personality?

Now you try it:

Write a paragraph that describes an animal you have seen and remember vividly. It can be a ragged, broken-down animal like the horse in the passage from "The Legend of Sleepy Hollow" or a beautiful, strong animal. Use specific imagery so that your reader can understand clearly what the animal looks like and what the animal's personality is like.

Irresistible Imagery

Student Lesson 11

Commentary and Suggestions for Teachers

Lesson Objective: to understand how imagery aids reading comprehension and to use imagery to make personal writing come alive

Consider the text:

This passage is a description of Ichabod Crane's horse. Ichabod Crane, one of the main characters in the story, is himself a comical, rundown figure. There have been many film versions and adaptations of "The Legend of Sleepy Hollow." Some of your students may have seen one or two adaptations. It would be interesting to read the original story and compare it to the film versions. Some vocabulary in this passage may be difficult: "bestrode" means rode. "Gaunt" is a word for extreme thinness. A "ewe" is a female sheep, and a "ewe neck" on a horse would be thick and short. "Spectral" means ghostly or supernatural. The horse's name is "Gunpowder," an indication that the horse has always had a bad temper.

Take a deeper look:

1. Pictures will vary; but they should include the horse's thinness, his thick neck, his messy coat, mane, and tail, and his glaring and gleaming eyes. It would be fun to post the pictures around the room to see if they differ.

2. The key to the horse's personality can be found in the visual image describing the horse's "good" eye: "the other [eye] had the gleam of a genuine devil in it." From this image, the reader knows that the horse has a vicious, wicked side equated with the devil himself.

Now you try it:

Students should first decide on an animal to describe and then do some prewriting in the form of a list or graphic organizer showing the specific images they will use to describe the animal's appearance and personality. As students write, remind them that the more specific the images are, the more vivid and alive the paragraphs will be. Have students share their paragraphs with a partner and see if the partner can draw the animal from the description.

Irresistible Imagery

Student Lesson 12

Consider the text:

In late 1838 they [the Cherokee Indians] left for the West. Some traveled by river. Most walked, and many were barefoot. The winter grew icy and bitter. They struggled to cross the frozen Mississippi River. Along the way they also battled drought, disease, hunger, and exhaustion.

Heather E. Schwartz, *Forced Removal: Causes and Effects of the Trail of Tears*

Take a deeper look:

1. This passage describes the forced removal of the Cherokee Indians from their ancestral land in the eastern United States to a harsh and unknown land in the West. Their journey is called the Trail of Tears because of all of the hardship and suffering the Cherokee had to endure on their forced march west. Read the passage several times, and think about the picture the author creates in your mind. What images from the passage do you remember most vividly? Why do you think you remember them so well?

2. Identify two images from the passage: one appealing to the sense of sight and one appealing to the sense of touch. What do these images add to your understanding of what happened to the Cherokee?

Now you try it:

Choose one of the details from the paragraph and develop it. Imagine traveling by river. What might that be like? Or what might it be like to walk barefoot in the winter? Write a few sentences describing what it would look like and feel like. Use at least one visual image and one touch image.

Irresistible Imagery

Student Lesson 12

Commentary and Suggestions for Teachers

<u>Lesson Objective:</u> to use sight and touch imagery to create a vivid experience for a reader

Consider the text:

This passage describes the forced removal of the Cherokee Indians from their ancestral land in the eastern United States to a harsh and unknown land in the West. Many, many of the Cherokee died along the way. This true story is one of the darkest moments in our history as a nation. Although the passage may be upsetting for some students, most students want to know the truth about our history. It helps us remember never to treat people in that way again. You may have to read this passage several times. Although the vocabulary is not difficult, the events may be troubling. Students may need some guidance and support.

Take a deeper look:

1. Answers will vary. This is a time for a serious discussion of the subject itself and of the power of language to help us understand the suffering of others.

2. Visual imagery includes "Most walked, and many were barefoot" and "They struggled to cross the frozen Mississippi River." Touch imagery includes "Most walked, and many were barefoot" and "The winter grew icy and bitter." The last line of the passage also brings to mind the intensity of the suffering. The images bring the readers into the scene. The specificity of the imagery helps readers understand that the pain and suffering of the Cherokee were not general and abstract. We can understand to some degree what they went through, seeing their suffering and feeling their pain.

Now you try it:

Students will need some time to think about this and talk about it. It would be helpful for them to do some prewriting here—a graphic organizer or a list of the images they want to include. Encourage students to use concrete images to help their readers visualize what is going on in the text. You may wish to work as a whole group with younger students.

Additional Resources for Irresistible Imagery

Irresistible Imagery Chart

Sense (sight, sound, touch, smell, or taste)	Specific Image

Examples and Nonexamples

Below are samples of text students can analyze to help them understand the importance of using imagery in their own writing. These examples and nonexamples allow students to:

- experience imagery as a powerful aid to comprehension,
- understand how authors use imagery to enhance meaning, and
- look at their own writing and see what they need to do to make the writing come alive.

Have students read all three examples and then use the chart to analyze the passages' use of imagery and explain why imagery is essential to quality writing.

Going to the Movies by N. Dean

Ex. 1: There were more than a hundred people trying to get into the movie theater. I thought we'd never get to the ticket booth. We had a good time, though. We finally got our tickets, got some popcorn, sat down, and enjoyed the movie.

Ex. 2: The movie theater was crowded, but it was fun.

Ex. 3: The line to buy tickets to the movie snaked around the block. There were all kinds of people in line: impatient children tugging on their parents' hands, trying to make the line go faster; teenagers with orange and blue hair, laughing and pretending that they couldn't care less if they got a ticket or not; and couples holding hands and whispering to each other. Finally, we got our tickets and entered the theater. The smell of popcorn hit us like a blast from a furnace. We got a large bin of popcorn and ate most of it before the movie started. The butter and salt stuck to our tongues and fingers and made us desperate for something to drink. Of course, we had to have a soft drink. We welcomed the cold fizz as we gulped and slurped our drinks. Then the movie came on. What a movie it was!

Abstract	Some Imagery	Alive with Imagery
Example number:	Example number:	Example number:
Why it doesn't work:	Why it's better but still not great:	Why it's the best:

The Swing by N. Danaher

Ex. 1: When another kid is on the swing at the park, it's worth the wait. When my turn finally comes, my mom gives me a gentle push to start and then I'm off—kicking my legs and pumping my arms to get higher and higher. When I go up I can touch the clear blue sky, and when I go down gravity tickles my stomach and I let out a giggle. Up and down and back and forth. I never want to get off!

Ex. 2: The swing is the best thing in the park. I can go really high!

Ex. 3: The swing is the best part about going to the park. Sometimes there is a line, but when it's my turn, I love to go as high as I can.

Abstract	Some Imagery	Alive with Imagery
Example number:	Example number:	Example number:
Why it doesn't work:	Why it's better but still not great:	Why it's the best:

Fabulous Figurative Language

Introduction

Metaphors, similes, personification, and hyperbole belong to a class of language called **figurative language**. Figurative language is any language that is **not** used in a literal way (meaning exactly what it says). It's a manner of saying one thing and meaning another. We use figurative language, or **figures of speech**, all of the time in spoken English. When we go to the grocery store, for example, we might make comments like these:

- This store is a freezer!
- The store is like a maze.
- That dark chocolate called out my name.
- There are thousands of choices in the cereal aisle.

If we look at these statements literally, they make no sense at all. The store is a store, not a freezer (even though it might be cold in the store). The store isn't a maze either (even though it may be hard to find things in the store). Dark chocolate cannot call out anyone's name; and although there are lots of cereal choices, there aren't thousands. Even though the statements make no literal sense at all, we understand them completely. That's because we've been using figurative language all of our lives! When someone says the store is a freezer, we understand that the store does not turn into a freezer. It is just very cold in the store. In the same way, the store is not a literal maze. But we know that it is easy to get lost in the twists and turns of a maze. We are saying that the grocery store's floor plan is hard to figure out. We also clearly understand that if dark chocolate is calling out my name, it simply means that I am very tempted to buy the dark chocolate. And the thousands of choices in the cereal aisle point out that there are many (but not thousands of) choices in the cereal aisle.

Why do we use figurative language? We use figurative language because it's a rich, strong, and vivid way to express meaning. By using figurative language, we are able to say much more in fewer words. Figures of speech compare two basically unlike objects or ideas. One is literal (what it is) and one is figurative (what it is not). The figurative object or idea helps us understand or picture the literal object or idea. Figurative language gives insight into the unfamiliar by comparing it to the familiar.

Sometimes it is difficult to separate figurative language from the other elements of voice (diction, detail, and imagery). That's because effective diction, detail, and imagery are used to create figurative language. But figurative language is different. If you describe a family gathering as "a combination of boisterous conversation, perfectly seasoned chicken, and the fragrance of freshly baked bread," you would be using effective diction, detail, and imagery but not figurative language. It describes the gathering exactly as it is, and there is no other meaning. If, however, you describe a family gathering as "a **quilt** of boisterous conversation, perfectly seasoned chicken, and the fragrance of freshly baked bread," you would be using diction, detail, imagery, **and** figurative language. A family gathering is not literally a quilt. It is **like** a quilt, combining different parts (here, sounds, smells, and tastes) to create the whole. Comparing the family gathering to a quilt here is a metaphor, and the metaphor is developed through diction, detail, and imagery.

There are several different kinds of figurative language. In this chapter we will explore four of the most important figures of speech: metaphors, similes, personification, and hyperbole.

Metaphors and Similes

Metaphors and similes are used to compare things that are not usually seen as similar. Metaphors **imply** the comparison, and similes **state** the comparison directly. Suppose you've just taken an extremely hard exam. To make this idea into a **metaphor**, you say, "That exam was a bear!" You are not saying that it was a literal bear but that it was unpredictable and hard to deal with. The comparison between the exam and a bear is not directly stated. Instead, the comparison is implied. You identify the bear with the exam. That's what a metaphor does. A metaphor implies a comparison to bring fresh, rich meaning to writing (and speaking).

A **simile** is a comparison, too. With a simile, however, the comparison is directly stated. To make the "exam" metaphor into a simile, you make the comparison explicit: "That exam was like struggling with a bear!" It is still nonliteral language—taking the exam is not really like struggling with a bear—but with a simile, you come right out and state the comparison. Similes have signal words that give you a hint a simile is coming. These words include *as, like, than, similar to*, and *resembles*. Be careful, though. These words don't always indicate similes. If I say, "I look like my sister," I am not using a simile. It's a literal statement; I *do* look like my sister. To be a simile or a metaphor, the comparison must be of essentially unlike things.

Metaphors and similes have **literal terms** and **figurative terms**. The **literal** term is what we are comparing to something else. It's what's real; it means what it is. For example, the literal term in the metaphor, "That exam was a bear!" is *exam*. We are really talking about an exam. The **figurative** term is what is being compared to the literal term. The figurative term means something other than itself, something nonliteral. The figurative term in the metaphor is *bear*. The exam is not a bear, but it has some bear-like qualities that can help us understand just how hard the exam was.

It is not essential to use these terms with students, but it helps. These concepts can help clarify the nature of figurative language, and it is difficult to understand and analyze figures of speech without them.

Personification

Another common figure of speech is **personification.** Personification is a special kind of metaphor that gives human qualities to something that is not human, such as a wild animal, an object, or an idea. For example, if we say, "The tree sighed sadly in the cold," we are using personification. A tree can't really sigh or be sad. We are giving the tree characteristics of a person. Personification, since it is a kind of metaphor, has a literal and figurative term. In this example, the literal term is the tree (it really is a tree) and the figurative term is a person (the tree is not a person, but the comparison gives the idea that the tree is in for a hard winter). In personification, the figurative term is always a person.

Hyperbole

A **hyperbole** (pronounced *hi per` bo lee*) is an exaggeration that is grounded in truth. The key to hyperboles is the part about truth. Hyperboles must be founded on truth to be meaningful. If I say, "I'm so tired I could sleep for a week," I am using a hyperbole. I'm not in a coma, and I couldn't really sleep for a week, but it feels that way. The truth lies in the extent of the tiredness. It's an exaggeration, but there is truth in it. Hyperboles add interest, sometimes humor, and emphasis to what you're trying to say. To be a hyperbole, the statement must be an exaggeration and not literally true.

Students in the elementary grades can learn to understand and write figures of speech. They can learn to pick out figurative language and understand the comparisons. They can learn to distinguish between figurative and literal terms. They can learn to write effective metaphors, similes, personification, and hyperboles. But it takes practice. That's what this chapter is about. These lessons will provide students with the tools they need in order to appreciate figurative language in reading and to use effective figures of speech in their own writing. For further support with literal and figurative language, you can use the Fabulous Figurative Language Chart on page 135 with any passage in this chapter.

The lessons are designed to progress in difficulty in terms of both the text students analyze and the activities students participate in. However, it is certainly not necessary to use every lesson or to go in a particular order. In addition, each lesson's commentary and suggestions for teachers are exactly that: suggestions that you may or may not use in your work with students. You are the experts. You know your kids. Our intent is only to provide support for very busy professionals.

Of note are some threads that run through all of the Fabulous Figurative Language lessons. First, it is important that students be able to see the passages that form the foundation of each lesson. You can run off individual copies of the passages. Alternatively, you can print them on chart paper or a whiteboard or project them. Another thread is the Literal and Fabulous Figurative Language Chart on page 136. This is a class charts for collecting figures of speech with literal and figurative terms from the lessons' passages and activities or in other texts. The chart should include figurative language that students find appealing. Finally, we have included additional practice with examples and nonexamples of how fabulous figurative language improves writing. This practice can be found on pages 137–138.

We hope these lessons are engaging and helpful for you and your students. With practice, students can learn the power of fabulous figurative language and go a long way toward finding their own voices.

> To help students feel comfortable with figurative language, it would be fun to have them interview parents or other adults about figurative phrases they use. There are some classic ones (***it rained cats and dogs, she's pretty as a picture, I could eat a horse***, etc.), but it might be interesting for students to see what other figures of speech adults use. It is always important to encourage the home-school connection.

Fabulous Figurative Language

Warm-up Lessons

The warm-up lessons are designed to introduce students to each element of voice. These lessons use simple text written to illustrate the specific element of voice under consideration—here, figurative language. The questions direct students' attention to the purpose and power of understanding figurative language in reading and using figurative language in writing. In addition, we provide a brief review of the importance of figurative language and suggest relevant academic language to include on word walls and in conversations with students.

Why figurative language is important:
- Figurative language helps the author express meaning in a strong, vivid way.
- Figurative language allows the author to say more in fewer words.
- Figurative language helps the reader understand the unfamiliar by comparing it with the familiar.
- Figurative language adds color and interest to the writing.

Warm-up 1

> Mockingbirds are the rulers of the sky. Any other bird that dares to invade their living space is chased away. The invader's size or shape does not matter. Mockingbirds will chase a red-shouldered hawk, a bird more than twice the size of a mockingbird, for a mile or more, the little monarch in hot pursuit of the fleeing hawk.
>
> T. W. Dean

1. What is the metaphor in this passage? What two things are compared? (The metaphor is "mockingbirds are rulers of the sky." Mockingbirds are compared to a king or queen—"the little monarch"—and the sky is compared to a kingdom.)

2. How does the metaphor help the reader understand the passage? (The metaphor compares the mockingbird, something readers may not know well, to something familiar, a king or queen. The comparison brings with it the sense of power and authority of an absolute monarch and emphasizes just how powerful and determined mockingbirds are. The metaphor is also extended. The monarch's kingdom, the sky, has "invaders," hawks and other birds. These birds are chased away by the "little monarch," the mockingbird.)

Warm-up 2

It was a hot day. As we walked along, the path felt like an oven. Our shoes melted as they touched the ground. The trees searched the sky for rain.

N. Dean

1. What is the simile in the passage? What two things are compared? (The simile is "the path felt like an oven." The path is compared to an oven, emphasizing how very hot it is.)

2. "Our shoes melted as they touched the ground" is an example of what figure of speech? (It is an example of hyperbole, exaggeration in the service of truth. The shoes don't really melt, but it is so hot it feels like the shoes are melting.)

3. "The trees searched the sky for rain" is an example of what figure of speech? (It is an example of personification. Trees can't really search for rain in the sky. Humans do that. The trees are being compared to people who search the sky for rain when it is very hot and dry.)

Word Wall Suggestions

figurative, literal, metaphor, simile, personification, hyperbole, explicit, implied

Fabulous Figurative Language

Student Lesson 1

Consider the text:

Trees and shrubs were becoming engulfed in a relentless wave of flame. Red-hot embers showered down on them, stinging their skin like vicious wasps.

J. Burchett and S. Vogler, ***Rainforest Rescue***

Take a deeper look:

1. What is the simile in this passage? What two things are being compared?

2. What does the simile tell you about how the hot embers feel?

Now you try it:

Pretend you are at the playground. The wind is blowing very hard and it is cold. Think about how the wind feels. What could you compare it to? Finish this sentence with a simile:

The cold wind felt like _____ .

Share your simile as your teacher writes it down.

Fabulous Figurative Language

Student Lesson 1

Commentary and Suggestions for Teachers

Lesson Objective: to understand how a simile works and to use similes in personal writing

Consider the text:

This passage is from a story that tells how two adventurous kids rescue an orangutan and save a nature preserve from greedy developers. In this scene, the kids are surrounded by a raging fire and barely escape. You will probably have to help students with some of the vocabulary: "Engulfed" here means surrounded; "relentless" means not stopping for anything; "embers" are hot sparks from the fire; and "vicious" means hurtful. Although the vocabulary may be a little challenging, the focus should be on the simile itself. Most students understand what an insect sting or bite feels like and will thus be able to thoroughly understand what the hot embers feel like to the characters in the story.

Take a deeper look:

1. The simile is in the second sentence: "Red-hot embers … [were] stinging their skin like vicious wasps." The simile compares what is actually there (the hot embers, the literal term) to something that is not there (the sting of vicious wasps, the figurative term) but makes the literal term clear. So the two things that are compared are the embers (the literal term) and the sting of vicious wasps (the figurative term). It is a simile because it is directly stated by coming right out and saying one thing is *like* another. What is important is that they understand the comparison, can recognize what is being compared, and can identify this as a simile.

2. By comparing the feeling of the hot embers on their skin to the sting of vicious wasps, the simile tells the reader (or listener) that the hot embers that land on the characters' skin are very painful. It is a sharp pain that lasts for quite a while, like the sting of a wasp. One of the values of similes (and metaphors) is that they help us understand the unfamiliar by comparing it to the familiar.

Now you try it:

Students can do this activity orally. Have them close their eyes and think of a cold, windy day on the playground. In small groups, have students talk about what the cold wind would feel like and what they could compare it to. Then each group can contribute a figurative term to a class discussion. If they are stuck, you might make some suggestions like these (figurative terms are underlined):

The cold wind felt like <u>someone dropping ice down my back.</u>

The cold wind felt like <u>a fan blowing snow on my face.</u>

The cold wind felt like <u>playing on the swings in a snowstorm.</u>

Fabulous Figurative Language

Student Lesson 2

Consider the text:

Some fish have a very keen sense of smell. Sharks have been described as "swimming noses." Up to two-thirds of a shark's brain may be involved in sensing smells. Its sense of smell is powerful enough to detect a single drop of blood in a swimming pool of water.

Robert Snedden, *Adaptation and Survival*

Take a deeper look:

1. Read or listen to the passage several times. What are sharks being compared to?

2. Why do you think the author makes the comparison between sharks and swimming noses?

Now you try it:

Draw a picture of a shark as a "swimming nose." Now think about another animal, a rabbit. Rabbits have excellent hearing and big ears. We could say that rabbits are hopping ears! Draw a picture of a rabbit as hopping ears.

Fabulous Figurative Language

Student Lesson 2

Commentary and Suggestions for Teachers

Lesson Objective: to understand how a metaphor works and how it is different from a simile

Consider the text:

Read the passage aloud several times. Explain that "keen" means powerful or sharp. In other words, sharks can smell things from very far away. See if students can put this passage in their own words. It can be simple, something like "sharks are really good at smelling things."

Take a deeper look:

1. Sharks are being compared to noses swimming in the water. Although it is not necessary, you might want to draw the distinction between a simile and a metaphor here. The figurative language in this passage is a simile because the comparison is directly stated: sharks "have been described as 'swimming noses.'" It is explicit. Note that similes are not always simply stated. The author doesn't say, "Sharks are like swimming noses." The meaning is the same, though. To be a metaphor, the author would have to say, "Sharks are swimming noses." This would be an implied comparison. The chart below may be helpful in clarifying the differences between similes, metaphors, and literal language.

Similes	Metaphors	Literal
• The shark is like a swimming nose. • The shark is similar to a swimming nose. • The shark resembles a swimming nose.	• The shark is a swimming nose. • The big nose swam through the water.	• The shark has a keener sense of smell than most other animals. • I like to watch a shark swimming in the aquarium.
• The rabbit is like a hopping ear. • The rabbit is nothing more than a hopping ear.	• The rabbit is a hopping ear. • The giant ears hopped through the grass.	• I like to watch rabbits hopping through the grass. • Rabbits have bigger ears than cats do.

2. By using this simile, the author is saying that the sense of smell is the most important sense the shark possesses. The sense of smell is so well developed and important that it almost seems like sharks are just noses swimming around in the water. It is a funny visual image, but the comparison also emphasizes how important the sense of smell is to a shark.

Now you try it:

Students can have fun drawing pictures of noses swimming around in the water. They could also include big shark teeth and shark fins and tails. Students can also have fun drawing a rabbit as hopping ears. The ears could have rabbit feet and a soft, fluffy rabbit tail. It would be helpful to post the pictures around the room for everyone to enjoy.

Fabulous Figurative Language

Student Lesson 3

Consider the text:

Hard, cold

rains lighten to

white, shimmering crystals.

Like a blanket, the snow covers

Us. Hush.

Jennifer Fandel, "The First Snowfall" from *Thorns, Horns, and Crescent Moons: Reading and Writing Nature Poems*

Take a deeper look:

1. Find the simile in the poem. What two things are being compared?

2. How does the simile add to your understanding of the poem?

Now you try it:

Complete the sentences below by writing similes. Remember that similes compare two things that are essentially **unlike** to help us clearly understand something.

Her smile was like _____ .

He ran like _____ .

The pencil was sharp as a _____ .

When you have written these similes, look back at some of your earlier writing. Where can you add a simile that will help your reader understand what you are writing about in a fresh and new way?

Fabulous Figurative Language

Student Lesson 3

Commentary and Suggestions for Teachers

Lesson Objective: to identify literal and figurative terms and to understand what similes add to our understanding of text

Consider the text:

The poem is about the first snowfall of the year. Read the poem aloud several times. If students live in a part of the country that doesn't get snow, it would be helpful to show them some pictures of snow-covered scenery. It would also be helpful to have students put the poem into their own words, so they understand the language of the poem.

Take a deeper look:

1. The simile is "Like a blanket, the snow covers / Us." The snow is compared to a blanket. "Snow" is the literal term and "blanket" is the figurative term. In other words, snow is snow. There is no real blanket. Snow is compared to a blanket to help us understand the feeling of the first snowfall, how it covers us like a blanket.

2. Snow is cold, but here it is compared to a blanket, which keeps us warm and comfortable. Yet the simile helps us get a clear picture of the snow, the exact picture the author intends. The snow is thick and smooth, like a blanket. It covers everything completely, the way a blanket covers someone. And it gives a feeling of quiet comfort, like a blanket. The author is not focusing on the negative aspects of snow, just snow's beauty and serenity.

Now you try it:

The similes should look something like this:

Her smile was like <u>sunshine after a storm</u>.

He ran like <u>the wind across the prairie</u>.

The pencil was sharp as <u>a needle</u>.

Remind students that similes compare two basically unlike objects or ideas. One is literal (what it actually is) and one is figurative (what it is not literally but is being compared to). The figurative object or idea helps us understand or picture the literal object or idea.

Have students look back at some of their earlier writing and find places to add similes. The similes should have clear literal and figurative terms and help readers understand the writing in a fresh and new way. Help students guard against false similes such as "I like ice cream" or "I work hard just like my brother does." Both of these examples are literal.

Fabulous Figurative Language

Student Lesson 4

Consider the text:

Scientists once thought T. rex stood upright like a kangaroo with its tail dragging behind. But most fossilized dinosaur tracks show no evidence of the tail dragging. Scientists now believe T. rex stood horizontal, like a teeter-totter. Its large, powerful tail on one end helped balance its huge head on the other end.

A. L. Wegwerth, *Tyrannosaurus Rex*

Take a deeper look:

1. What are the two similes in the passage? What two things are compared in each simile?

2. How do the similes help you understand the passage?

Now you try it:

Think of a pet you have had or an animal you have seen in the zoo or a park. Talk about this animal with a partner. Now write about the animal. Write in such a way as to help your partner "see" the animal just the way you do. Include at least one simile. Read what you have written to your partner. As your partner listens, he or she should draw what he or she hears and then share it with you. Discuss how the drawing compares to your understanding of the animal. Does your partner picture the animal the same way you do?

Fabulous Figurative Language

Student Lesson 4

Commentary and Suggestions for Teachers

Lesson Objective: to use similes to compare the unfamiliar to the familiar in order to help the reader fully understand what is written

Consider the text:

This passage is from a book about Tyrannosaurus rex. The passage focuses on the way T. rex stands. If students are unfamiliar with this dinosaur, it would be helpful to show them some pictures, readily available on the Internet. Depending of their level of background knowledge, you might also need to show them pictures of kangaroos. A teeter-totter is the same thing as a seesaw, a term students might be more familiar with.

Take a deeper look:

1. The first simile is "T. rex stood upright like a kangaroo with its tail dragging behind." The old view of the way T. rex stood (something unfamiliar) is compared to the stance of a kangaroo (something more familiar). The second simile is "T. rex stood horizontal, like a teeter-totter." The new view of the way T. rex stood (something unfamiliar) is compared to a teeter-totter or seesaw (something familiar).

2. The similes help the reader understand the changing views of how T. rex stood. We can picture the two stances because of the comparison of something unfamiliar (how T. rex stood) with something familiar (first the kangaroo and then the seesaw).

Now you try it:

Sentences will vary according to the animal students chose. The part to stress in this activity is the simile. Students should first spend time thinking about the animal and deciding what simile to use. Then they should spend some time writing. When they are done, they should read what they have written to their partners. As partners listen, they should draw in a notebook or on a whiteboard what they hear. The partners will then reveal what they have drawn, and the author and partner will discuss how accurate the drawing turned out. This will help students see how important the unfamiliar/familiar connection is.

Fabulous Figurative Language

Student Lesson 5

Consider the text:

The wolves were now more open in their pursuit, trotting sedately behind and ranging along on either side, their red tongues lolling out, their lean sides showing the undulating ribs with every movement. They were very lean, mere skin-bags stretched over bony frames, with strings for muscles—so lean that Henry found it in his mind to marvel that they still kept their feet and did not collapse forthright in the snow.

Jack London, ***White Fang***

Take a deeper look:

1. Find an example of a metaphor in the passage. Remember that two things are being compared in a metaphor. What two things are being compared? What do we learn about the wolves by comparing them to something that is not the wolves?

2. How would the feeling of the passage change if London had written the second sentence like this? **"The wolves were very skinny."**

Now you try it:

Think about two dogs you have seen in your neighborhood. Now think carefully about how a metaphor can help other people picture the dogs clearly. Fill in the chart below with something that identifies the dog, something the dog is, and something you compare the dog to. One has been done for you as an example.

Identify the dog	What the dog is	What you could compare the dog to
The little fuzzy dog that barks all of the time	A yapping dog	A furry noisemaker at a birthday party

Fabulous Figurative Language

Student Lesson 5

Commentary and Suggestions for Teachers

Lesson Objective: to use metaphors to express meaning in a powerful way

Consider the text:

White Fang, the title character, is half wolf, half dog. Most of the story, which tells of White Fang's gradually learning to trust humans, is told from the wolf-dog's point of view. This passage takes place in the Yukon Territory, Canada, where it is very cold and wild. Wolves are stalking Henry and Bill, two of the characters in the novel. Have students read the passage several times (or read the passage aloud to them), thinking about what the metaphors are and what they add to the passage. There may be some vocabulary you have to clarify: "sedately" (calmly), "ranging" (going), "lolling" (dangling), "undulating" (rippling), "marvel" (to wonder).

Take a deeper look:

1. There are two metaphors in this passage: the wolves are "skin-bags stretched over bony frames" and their muscles are "strings." We learn just how skinny and starving the wolves are through the metaphors. The wolves are "mere skin-bags," with no flesh on their bones at all. Their muscles are "string," so thin they barely seem like muscles at all. The emphasis on how starving the wolves are increases the tension between the predators (wolves) and the prey (sled dogs and men) and shows just how fierce and desperate the wolves are.

2. Without the metaphors and the accompanying detail, the reader has no concrete idea of what the wolves are like. They are just skinny. The reader loses the sense of fear and desperation that the original sentence has. The tension and interest are gone.

Now you try it:

This is the fundamental work of metaphor writing. The focus of the example is on how noisy the dog is and how annoying the noise is. Students can focus on what the dog looks like, sounds like, or even smells like. Be certain they understand that the dog is a dog. What they compare the dog to gives the reader an understanding of what the dog is like.

Fabulous Figurative Language

Student Lesson 6

Consider the text:

The [British] troops were there to protect the colonists from future attacks from the French or American Indians. They were also there to stop colonists from moving west. These new restrictions planted the first seeds of ill feeling between colonists and Great Britain.

Kassandra Radomski, *Battle for a New Nation: Causes and Effects of the Revolutionary War*

Take a deeper look:

1. Explanatory text uses figurative language, too. Figurative language helps us understand information by connecting what we are learning to what we already know. "The first seeds of ill feeling" is a metaphor. The "first seeds" are being compared to a beginning. Why do you think the author uses a metaphor instead of just saying, "the beginnings of ill feeling"?

2. Why is "the first seeds of ill feeling" a metaphor and not a simile?

Now you try it:

Complete the following sentences with metaphors. Remember that a metaphor is a comparison of essentially unlike things, but the comparison gives us new understanding and insight. The first one is done for you.

The lake was a mirror.

My room is _____ .

My best friend is _____ .

Cafeteria food is _____ .

Share your sentences with the class. When you are finished, look back at some of the writing you have done before and see where you can add metaphors to make your writing clearer and stronger.

Fabulous Figurative Language

Student Lesson 6

Commentary and Suggestions for Teachers

Lesson Objective: to understand the importance of metaphors in informational writing

Consider the text:

This is informational text about the Revolutionary War. Informational text uses figurative language to clarify ideas and make the detail more interesting. Here we have a metaphor with an implied literal term. The British didn't literally plant "first seeds of ill feeling." The "seeds" are figurative. The ***beginning*** (the literal term) of ill feeling is compared to the "first seeds."

Take a deeper look:

1. The author uses a metaphor to clarify and intensify meaning. Beginnings are just beginnings. Seeds, however, grow. By using a metaphor, the author is able to show that the ill feelings started from the restrictions; and she is also able to imply that the ill feeling will sprout and grow, like a seed: The ill feelings will intensify.

2. "The first seeds of ill feeling" is a metaphor, not a simile, since it does not use the words "as," "like," "similar to," or any expression that makes the comparison explicitly clear. Instead, the comparison is implied, which is characteristic of a metaphor.

Now you try it:

Sentences will vary. If students have trouble thinking of metaphors, you can share some of the examples below with them.

The lake was a mirror. (Other ideas: a dragon, a mad dog, a warm bath)

My room is _____ . (Ideas: a tornado, an ice cube, a fort)

My best friend is _____ . (Ideas: a rock, a warm blanket, a volcano)

The playground is _____ . (Ideas: a zoo, a roller coaster, a battlefield)

Once students have practiced with metaphors, have them look at their previous writing to see where they can add metaphors to clarify and intensify meaning.

Fabulous Figurative Language

Student Lesson 7

Consider the text:

He was tall, but exceedingly lank, with narrow shoulders, long arms and legs, hands that dangled a mile out of his sleeves, feet that might have served for shovels, and his whole frame most loosely hung together. His head was small, and flat at top, with huge ears, large green glassy eyes, and a long snipe nose, so that it looked like a weather-cock perched upon his spindle neck to tell which way the wind blew.

Washington Irving, "The Legend of Sleepy Hollow"

Take a deeper look:

1. This passage describes Ichabod Crane, one of the main characters in "The Legend of Sleepy Hollow." This passage contains lots of figurative language. Find an example of each of the following figures of speech: hyperbole, metaphor, and simile. To do this, you will need a copy of the text and three colored pencils. Follow along as your teacher reads the passage aloud. Then make a key with your colored pencils (for example, hyperbole is green, metaphor is pink, and simile is blue). Circle or underline the figures of speech in the appropriate color. Check in with a partner to see if you are on track. Then discuss the results with your teacher and class.

2. How does the figurative language help you understand this passage?

Now you try it:

Write a sentence that contains an example of hyperbole. Start your sentence like this:

He hit the ball so far it _____ .

Fabulous Figurative Language

Student Lesson 7

Commentary and Suggestions for Teachers

Lesson Objective: to identify examples of hyperbole, metaphor, and simile and to explain what the figurative language adds to meaning

Consider the text:

Ichabod Crane is one of the main characters in the story. He is a comical, rundown figure, described vividly in this passage. Some vocabulary in this passage may be difficult for students: "lank" (very thin); "frame" (here, his body); "snipe" (a wading bird with a long, thin bill); "weather-cock" (a movable statue of a rooster that is mounted on a roof to show wind direction); "spindle" (a pole for spinning thread). Once students understand the vocabulary, they will be able to pick out the figurative language.

Take a deeper look:

1. These are the examples of figurative language in the passage:

Hyperbole: "hands that dangled a mile out of his sleeves"; "feet that might have served for shovels"

These examples are both exaggeration in the service of truth. The hands don't really dangle a mile and his feet are not as big as shovels. The hyperboles help the reader understand that his arms are very long and his feet are very big. The hyperboles add interest and precision of expression to the description.

Metaphor: "green glassy eyes"; "a long snipe nose"; "spindle neck"

The first metaphor compares his eyes to green glass (without depth or expression). The second metaphor implies that his nose is like the long, thin beak of a wading bird. The third metaphor implies that his neck was like a pole or stick. The metaphors help us fully understand what Ichabod Crane looks like.

Simile: "it looked like a weather-cock perched upon his spindle neck to tell which way the wind blew"

This long simile compares his entire head to a weather-cock on a pole blowing this way and that way, according to the direction of the wind. It is a simile since it is directly stated. The simile helps the reader understand just how odd Ichabod Crane looks.

2. The figurative language brings the passage to life and helps us clearly visualize Ichabod Crane. If the author had just said that the character was thin and funny looking, we would really have very little idea of what Ichabod Crane looks like. The figurative language brings precision to the visual imagery by adding all of the extra information contained in the figurative terms of the hyperboles, metaphors, and simile.

Now you try it:

Here are a few examples that can help students understand the power of hyperboles.

He hit the ball so far it <u>hit the ice in Antarctica</u>.

He hit the ball so far it <u>landed on a mountain 20 miles away</u>.

He hit the ball so far it <u>bounced off a whale in the middle of the ocean</u>.

Give students an opportunity to share their sentences.

Fabulous Figurative Language

Student Lesson 8

Consider the text:

> Air resistance works against road-racing cyclists. To cut down on air resistance and ride their fastest, cyclists wear tight shorts and fitted jerseys. Some top riders even have their jerseys specially tailored so they fit like a second skin.

> Suzanne Slade, *The Science of Bicycle Racing*

Take a deeper look:

1. Science books use figurative language, too. They use similes and metaphors to help us understand the science by comparing science concepts to things that are familiar to us. This passage is from a book that discusses the science of bicycle racing. In this passage, the author is talking about air resistance and the clothes cyclists wear to reduce air resistance. The author uses a simile. Identify the simile.

2. What two things are being compared in this simile? How does the simile help us understand the way the cyclists' jerseys fit?

Now you try it:

Think of a sport that requires a special uniform or specific clothing. It could be football, soccer, baseball, volleyball, track, hockey, or basketball—any sport you are familiar with. Now write an introductory sentence and a simile to help others understand more about this article of clothing. Use Slade's passage as a model. Below is another example to help you get the right idea.

Motorcycling requires special gear to keep the rider protected. Many riders wear padding inside their jackets that works like armor to protect them if they fall.

Fabulous Figurative Language

Student Lesson 8

Commentary and Suggestions for Teachers

Lesson Objective: to understand the power of figurative language in informational text

Consider the text:

Have students read the passage several times. It would be helpful to briefly explain air resistance (the force of the air against a moving object). The faster the object is moving, the more resistance there is. This is why bicycle racers want clothes that reduce air resistance. They want to go fast **and** cut down air resistance so it does not slow them down. "Tailored" here means made to measure.

Take a deeper look:

1. The simile is "they [the jerseys] fit like a second skin." It is a simile because it is directly stated (here, using "like").

2. In this simile, the specially tailored jerseys are compared to a second skin. The jerseys are what they are (the literal term) and the second skin is not really a second skin but tells us what the jerseys are like (it is the figurative term). The jerseys are so close fitting and smooth that they are similar to another layer of skin instead of just a jersey. The simile helps the reader picture the jerseys and understand what they look and feel like.

Now you try it:

First, have students talk about this with a partner to get ideas. Then they can work on their two sentences. The models should help them write their sentences. It would be beneficial to have students share their sentences with the class. Check to be sure that they use a simile and not literal description. Of course, if they use a metaphor instead of a simile, that is fine.

As an alternative activity, you could have students describe the uniforms as if the athlete were participating in a fashion show. It would be an engaging way to be descriptive. Students would have to use a simile (or metaphor) to explain the clothing. You could even provide pictures from the Internet of famous athletes in their uniforms, and students would have to write commentary, using metaphors and similes, for a "fashion show."

Fabulous Figurative Language

Student Lesson 9

Consider the text:

> I saw you toss the kites on high
>
> And blow the birds about the sky;
>
> And all around I heard you pass,
>
> Like ladies' skirts across the grass—
>
> > O wind, a-blowing all day long,
> >
> > O wind, that sings so loud a song!
>
> Robert Louis Stevenson, "The Wind"

Take a deeper look:

1. In this poem, the wind is personified, given human characteristics. Give one example from the poem of personification of the wind.

2. Find an example of a simile in the poem and explain what two things are being compared.

Now you try it:

Write a sentence that contains an example of personification. Start your sentence like this:

My homework _____ .

Fabulous Figurative Language

Student Lesson 9

Commentary and Suggestions for Teachers

<u>Lesson Objective:</u> to identify and write examples of personification

Consider the text:

In this stanza from Stevenson's poem, the speaker of the poem is directly addressing the wind. He talks to the wind as if it were a person, personification in itself. Read the stanza several times so that students can pick out the examples of personification and simile. It also would be helpful to review what personification and simile are and how they are figurative, not literal.

Take a deeper look:

1. Examples of personification include

- "I saw [the wind] toss the kites on high"
- "I saw [the wind] blow the birds about the sky"
- "O wind … that sings so loud a song!"

The wind is given human characteristics: it tosses kites about and blows birds around purposefully, as if it is human, willful and determined. In addition, the wind "sings" a loud song, human behavior attributed to the wind. Any of these examples are acceptable. Personification helps the reader understand the nature of the wind exactly as the poet intends.

2. The simile in this poem is "I heard you pass, / Like ladies' skirts across the grass." The sound of the wind is being compared to the sound of long skirts sweeping across the grass. We understand the sound of the wind by comparing it to something we can readily understand. The simile makes the poem's imagery more concrete and vivid. It is a simile because it is directly stated, using the word "like."

Now you try it:

Here are a few examples that can help students understand the power of personification:

My homework <u>hit me in the stomach</u>.

My homework <u>sat up and shook hands with me</u>.

My homework <u>tied me up and kept me captive for the afternoon</u>.

Divide students into groups and have them share their sentences. Each group can select a favorite sentence and share it with the class.

As an alternative activity, have students pick their favorite school supply and write an example of personification about it. An example might be: **My pencil stood at attention, ready to follow my orders.**

Fabulous Figurative Language

Student Lesson 10

Consider the text:

A campfire needs logs, branches, or paper to keep burning. The flames go out when the fire runs out of its energy source. Just like a fire, your body burns fuel. You have to feed the fire inside you with food.

Dana Meachen Rau, *Sports Nutrition for Teen Athletes: Eat Right to Take Your Game to the Next Level*

Take a deeper look:

1. This entire passage uses figurative language to explain your body's need for food. Fill in the missing blanks in the following chart to help you understand how the figurative language works.

Figure of speech	What it is (literal term)	What it is compared to (figurative term)	Metaphor or simile?
your body is like a fire	your body		
"your body burns fuel"		a fire that burns fuel	
"you have to feed the fire inside you"	the body's need for something that provides energy		metaphor
food is fuel		fuel	

2. How does thinking about a campfire help you understand the body's need for food?

Now you try it:

Complete the sentences below. Fill in the blanks in order to write a simile and show what you think friendship is like.

Friendship is like a _____ .

Just as a _____ needs_____ , friendship needs_____.

Here is an example to help you get started.

Friendship is like a <u>flower</u>. Just as a <u>flower</u> needs <u>sunshine</u>, friendship needs <u>honesty.</u>

Here, friendship is compared to a flower (a simile), and the need for honesty in friendship is compared to a flower's need for sunshine (another simile).

Fabulous Figurative Language

Student Lesson 10

Commentary and Suggestions for Teachers

Lesson Objective: to identify and write literal and figurative terms of similes and metaphors

Consider the text:

Informational text uses figurative language to explain by comparing the familiar to a new or difficult concept. Here the central simile compares a campfire and its need for fuel to the body and its need for food. Be certain students understand the central simile before they complete the chart or answer any questions.

Take a deeper look:

1. The chart should look something like this:

Figure of speech	What it is (literal term)	What it is compared to (figurative term)	Metaphor or simile?
your body is like a fire	your body	a fire	simile
"your body burns fuel"	your body's use of food	a fire that burns fuel	metaphor
"you have to feed the fire inside you"	the body's need for something that provides energy	feeding the fire with fuel	metaphor
food is fuel	food	fuel	metaphor

If students are not able to fill in every part of the chart, that's fine—as long as they understand the basic simile ("your body is like a fire"). Some of the metaphors are tricky, with understood or implied literal or figurative terms. As long as they get the idea that the body and its need for food are being compared to a fire and its need for fuel, they are fine.

2. The figurative language helps students understand the body's need for food by comparing it to something familiar, something that is easy to observe and understand. Without fuel, a fire goes out. In the same way, the body cannot function without food. The comparison helps students clearly see the need for the body's fuel: food.

Now you try it:

Sentences will vary. If students are stuck, let them read the example several times and talk about the assignment for a few minutes. Students can help each other think about friendship. Let students share their sentences and their thoughts about friendship after they have completed their two sentences.

Fabulous Figurative Language

Student Lesson 11

Consider the text:

The tiger's roar filled the cave with thunder. Mother Wolf shook herself clear of the cubs and sprang forward, her eyes, like two green moons in the darkness, facing the blazing eyes of Shere Khan.

Rudyard Kipling, *The Jungle Book*

Take a deeper look:

1. Read the first sentence again. What is the metaphor in the sentence? What two things are being compared? Why do you think the author uses a metaphor instead of a literal description?

2. There is a metaphor and a simile in the second sentence. What are they? How does the figurative language help you visualize the scene?

Now you try it:

Complete sentence one with a simile and sentence two with a metaphor.

1. **When she is mad, my teacher's voice is like** _____ .

2. **When my teacher is very happy, her voice is** _____ .

Fabulous Figurative Language

Student Lesson 11

Commentary and Suggestions for Teachers

Lesson Objective: to understand and explain the power of using figurative language in writing

Consider the text:

Students may be familiar with this story. They may have read the book or watched the Disney movie. This passage is from the beginning of **The Jungle Book**, when Mowgli (an orphaned human child) comes to live with the wolves. Here the mother wolf is protecting Mowgli from Shere Khan, a tiger who is Mowgli's sworn enemy. An understanding of this passage will help students see the power of figurative language.

Take a deeper look:

1. The metaphor is essentially the entire first sentence: "The tiger's roar filled the cave with thunder." Specifically, the metaphor states that the roar *is* thunder (meaning, of course, it is *like* thunder). The two things being compared are the roar and thunder. With this metaphor, the author is able to convey the power and force of the roar. Thunder is not only loud, but it is also frightening and awe-inspiring. It can make animals run for cover and can even make a house shake. The metaphor says it all. With one word, "thunder," the author brings a rich and complex meaning to the sentence.

2. The metaphor is the "blazing eyes of Shere Khan." The author is comparing the tiger's eyes to a blazing fire or even the sun. The simile is "her eyes [were] like two green moons in the darkness," comparing the mother wolf's eyes to two green moons. The figurative language (both the metaphor and the simile) helps the reader see the mother wolf's eyes and the tiger's eyes clearly and distinctly. The wolf's eyes are not merely green. They are mysterious, like the moon, shining with a strange inner light. They are cool but determined, shining with inner strength in the darkness. The tiger's eyes, in contrast, are "blazing." This is a fire more like the sun. There is no mystery there, only a threatening, bullying power.

Now you try it:

If students have trouble thinking of similes and metaphors, you can share these examples with them.

1. When she is mad, my teacher's voice is like the squawk of a crow, the honking of a horn in traffic, the roar of a lion, a crashing wave on the shore.

2. When my teacher is very happy, her voice is sunshine, light rain on a summer day, wind chimes on a spring morning, a song.

Fabulous Figurative Language

Student Lesson 12

Consider the text:

King's powerful words rang in the nation's ears. His speech inspired people to keep fighting for civil rights.

Lori Mortensen, *Voices of the Civil Rights Movement: A Primary Source Exploration of the Struggle for Racial Equality*

Take a deeper look:

1. This passage describes a speech by Dr. Martin Luther King Jr., a very important person in the civil rights movement. This speech was powerful and helped convince people that everyone, not just white people, should have equal rights in this country. To emphasize the power of this particular speech, the author uses personification. Identify the personification in this passage.

2. How does the use of personification help the reader fully understand this passage?

Now you try it:

Make a list of different sports or games you know well and the equipment and actions related to the sport or game. Now help your reader understand something about the sport or game you choose by using personification. Remember that with personification you have to give the nonhuman thing you are talking about human characteristics. Here are some examples to get you started:

The bat jumped out of her hands when she hit the ball. (The bat is being compared to a person jumping. A bat, as you know, can't really jump. The idea is to help the reader see that the bat is thrown so hard that it looks like it actually has a human life of its own.)

The ball smiled as it sank into the net. (Of course, the ball can't smile. It is being compared to a person who smiles. The idea here is that the ball goes into the net so perfectly it seems to smile.)

Fabulous Figurative Language

Student Lesson 12

Commentary and Suggestions for Teachers

Lesson Objective: to compare two objects/ideas through personification.

Consider the text:

It would be helpful to provide some background knowledge about Dr. Martin Luther King Jr. and the civil rights movement. Share the fact that Dr. King was a powerful speaker and that he advocated non-violent protest. His work changed how America thought about civil rights and paved the path to the Civil Rights Act of 1964, which made segregation illegal.

Take a deeper look:

1. The personification in this passage is found in the first sentence. The nation (America) is personified by the reference to "the nation's ears." A nation, of course, cannot have ears. It is giving human characteristics to something nonhuman. The consciousness or awareness of the people in the nation is compared to the ears of a person.

2. By personifying the nation's understanding and awareness (calling them "the nation's ears"), the author emphasizes the profound effect Dr. King's words had on the people of our country. The words "rang in the nation's ears" compare his words to a bell or chime (here a metaphor) and suggest (through the personification) that everyone in the country heard his words. The personification helps the reader understand the power of Dr. King's words and the importance of his message for all Americans.

Now you try it:

Have students read the examples several times. Then give them time to think about their own examples of personification. This activity would work well with partner groups.

Additional Resources for Fabulous Figurative Language

Fabulous Figurative Language Chart

Figure of Speech	What Kind? (Metaphor, Simile, Personification)	Literal Term	Figurative Term

Literal and Figurative Language Chart

This chart is another resource you can use to help students with literal and figurative language. It can be used as support with any of the passages in this chapter or as support with any text.

What the text explicitly says	What the author means
Example: Our shoes melted as they touched the ground.	Example: The ground was very hot.

Examples and Nonexamples

Below are samples of text students can analyze to help them understand the importance of using figurative language in their own writing. These examples and nonexamples allow students to:

- experience figurative language as a powerful aid to comprehension,
- understand how authors use figurative language to enhance meaning, and
- look at their own writing and see what they need to do to make the writing come alive.

Have students read all three examples and then use the chart to analyze the passages' use of figurative language and explain why figurative language is essential to quality writing.

Reading by N. Dean

Ex. 1: Reading is fun. I really like to read.

Ex. 2: Reading takes me places I have never been before. It is like being in another country.

Ex. 3: Reading is a train that takes me where I want to go. If I want to laugh, I sit in the comedy car, the one that tells jokes. I laugh until my stomach bursts and more laughter falls merrily on the floor. If I want to be scared, I sit in the mystery car. I slink down in my seat like a scared cat and shiver as I hear all about the danger of walking alone in the woods at night. I am quiet as a bell without a clapper. Every sound scares me. If I want to learn something new, I sit in the information car. I learn about the world: that after winter, spring can creep up gently and wrap you in comforting warmth just like the smile of a good friend after a bad day.

Text	Figurative Language	Effect on the Reader
Ex. 1		
Ex. 2		
Ex. 3		

Garbage Night by N. Danaher

Ex. 1: I don't like taking out the garbage. It's my least favorite chore.

Ex. 2: The worst chore is taking out the garbage. It's heavy, and it smells bad.

Ex. 3: It's Tuesday, and I know what that means—garbage night. I open the lid to the garbage can and feel the hot, smelly air touch my face. It's like a monster's breath as he laughs at how disgusted I am. I slam the lid shut and run back inside, fast as a cheetah, telling myself that I don't have to do that again … until next Tuesday.

Text	Figurative Language	Effect on the Reader
Ex. 1		
Ex. 2		
Ex. 3		

Tricky Tone

Introduction

Tone is the expression of the author's **attitude** toward his or her audience and subject matter. It can also be the expression of a narrator's or a character's attitude toward his or her reader or subject matter. And sometimes it's a little of both. There are as many different tones as there are attitudes: serious, lighthearted, playful, sarcastic, accepting, and so forth. The trick is to be able to identify tone in reading and create tone in writing.

It's easy to identify tone in spoken language. If a friend has been waiting at a restaurant for a half hour for you to show up and she says, "Oh, I love sitting alone and waiting," you know exactly what she means. She does not like waiting alone, and she does not like for you to be late. You understand her tone all too well: She is annoyed with you. We understand tone in speech by listening not only to words but also to the way words are said and the facial expressions and body language of those who say them.

Understanding tone will not be a new concept for students, although they might not know the term, **tone**. When you think about it, children learn to distinguish tone at a very young age. If a parent calls a child's name in a particular way, the child quickly understands if the parent is angry, happy, proud, or anxious— just by the tone of voice. It's not what is said but how it's said, the attitude behind the speech. Children learn this through experience.

Understanding tone in reading and creating tone in writing can be tricky. This is because a reader can't depend on vocal and facial expressions. Nevertheless, good readers learn to understand tone in what they read. Just as we understand tone in speech from what is said and how it is said, we understand tone in reading from what is written and how it's written. And as we learn to master tone in reading, we become more and more able to create a specific tone in our own writing. It just takes practice.

As you introduce tone to your students, it is helpful to connect it to purpose and audience. Having a clear purpose helps an author determine the exact tone he or she wants to create. If, for example, an author's purpose is to amuse, he or she may create a tone that is playful and humorous. Or if an author's purpose is to convince, he or she may create a confident or critical tone. Tone depends on purpose.

Tone also depends on audience. If the audience is a group of thoughtful scientists, an author would not create a silly or humorous tone. Instead, the author would create a serious or informative tone, a tone that suits the audience. If, on the other hand, the audience is a group of nine-year-old children who love to laugh, an author would strive for a tone that is comical or even silly. Tone depends on audience.

It is also helpful to connect tone to **point of view** or opinion. Tone supports point of view. If an author's point of view is that cell phones should never be allowed in school, the tone would probably be critical and judgmental. If, however, the author advocates the use of cell phones in school for both research and communication, the tone would probably be enthusiastic and sympathetic. Point of view and tone go hand in hand.

To identify tone, students must learn to read closely and carefully and to look for evidence in the text. Authors create tone in writing through the elements of voice: diction, detail, figurative language, and imagery. Good readers look closely at these elements. It is through the elements of voice that authors design how something is said. As students get better and better at recognizing the power of word choice, the selection of specific detail, the use of imagery, and the insights of figurative language, they will find the keys to understanding how tone helps readers understand the deep meaning of text. And as students come to understand the tone of what they read, they will become more skilled in creating a tone of their own.

As you work with the tone exercises that follow, students will need to practice several skills:

- identifying the **purpose** of a text;
- recognizing the intended **audience** of a text;
- understanding the **point of view** of a text;
- figuring out the **tone** of a text;
- explaining how they know the tone of a passage by careful attention to the **evidence** in the text, especially the **elements of voice**; and
- writing passages in which they identify a purpose, audience, and point of view and **create an appropriate tone** to suit that purpose, audience, and point of view.

All of these skills will get easier with practice. To discuss tone, students need to develop a **tone vocabulary**. On the next page is a beginning list of tone words. As you discuss the tone of passages here and in your other reading, keep adding to the list. (The Tone Words Chart is reprinted at the end of this chapter on page 175.)

Tone Words Chart

accepting	disrespectful	neutral	Additional Tone Words
admiring	doubtful	objective	
affectionate	enthusiastic	peaceful	
angry	fearful	playful	
anxious	forceful	questioning	
approving	frightening	reproachful	
bitter	harsh	respectful	
bristling	haughty	sad	
calm	humorous	sarcastic	
cold	impartial	serious	
comical	indifferent	sharp	
complementary	informative	silly	
confident	joyful	straightforward	
confused	judgmental	sympathetic	
contemptuous	lighthearted	thoughtful	
critical	loving	threatening	
detached	mistrustful	uncertain	
didactic	mocking	whimsical	
disdainful	mysterious		

Understanding tone can be tricky, but it is worth the effort. When students understand tone, they can connect to the author's deep and sometimes unstated meaning. That's what reading is all about! With an understanding of and practice with tone, students can learn to capture tone in their own writing, adding richness of meaning to their work. And that's what writing's all about!

These lessons are designed to progress in difficulty in terms of both the text students analyze and the activities students participate in. However, it is certainly not necessary to use every lesson or to go in a particular order. In addition, each lesson's commentary and suggestions for teachers are exactly that: suggestions that you may or may not use in your work with students. You are the experts. You know your kids. Our intent is only to provide support for very busy professionals.

Of note are some threads that run through all of the Tricky Tone lessons. First, it is important that students be able to see the passages that form the foundation of each lesson. You can run off individual copies of the passages. Alternatively, you can print them on chart paper or a whiteboard or project them. Another thread is the Tone Words Chart. This is a class chart of words to describe tone that students collect from the lessons' passages and activities. There is a chart you can use at the end of this chapter on page 175. Finally, we have included additional practice with examples and nonexamples of how tone improves writing. This practice can be found on pages 176–177.

We hope these lessons are engaging and helpful for you and your students. With practice, students can learn the power of tricky tone and go a long way toward finding their own voices.

Tricky Tone

Warm-up Lessons

The warm-up lessons are designed to introduce students to each element of voice. These lessons use simple text written to illustrate the specific element of voice under consideration—here, tone. The questions direct students' attention to the purpose and power of understanding tone in reading and crafting tone in writing. In addition, we provide a brief review of the importance of tone and suggest relevant academic language to include on word walls and in conversations with students.

Why tone is important:
- Understanding tone helps readers understand the deep meaning of text.
- Creating tone in writing helps students master the other elements of voice (word choice, detail, imagery, and figurative language) and adds richness and meaning to their work.
- Tone reflects the author's purpose and audience.
- Tone reveals the author's attitude and point of view.

Warm-up 1

> Understanding tone in reading and creating tone in writing can be tricky. This is because readers can't depend on voice and facial expressions. Nevertheless, good readers learn to understand tone in what they read. Just as we understand tone in speech from what is said and how it is said, we understand tone in reading from what is written and how it's written. And as we learn to master tone in reading, we become more and more able to create a specific tone in our own writing. It just takes practice.
>
> N. Dean

1. What is the purpose of this passage? (to inform or explain)

2. Who is the audience? (students who are learning how to identify tone in reading and create tone in their own writing)

3. What is the tone? (straightforward and informative)

Warm-up 2

I saw that guy trip my best friend Sal. I saw it! And it wasn't the first time. That guy has stuffed trash in Sal's locker, texted mean messages to Sal, and made fun of him any chance he gets. I felt the fire rise from my gut to the top of my head. I wanted to explode! This was the last straw. The bullying stops today!

N. Dean

1. What is the purpose of the passage? (to describe a situation and express emotion)

2. What is the tone? (angry)

3. How is the tone created? Look at the examples of word choice, detail, imagery, and figurative language for examples.

[Word choice: "that guy," "fire," "gut," "explode," and "bullying"

Detail: "That guy has stuffed trash in Sal's locker, texted mean messages to Sal, and made fun of him any chance he gets." And "I felt the fire rise from my gut to the top of my head. I wanted to explode!"

Imagery: "I saw that guy trip my best friend Sal." (sight), "stuffed trash in Sal's locker, texted mean messages to Sal, and made fun of him any chance he gets." (sight and sound), "I felt the fire rise from my gut to the top of my head." (touch)

Figurative language: "fire" (metaphor), "I wanted to explode!" (hyperbole), "This was the last straw." (metaphor)]

Word Wall Suggestions

tone, attitude, purpose, audience, point of view, evidence

Tricky Tone

Student Lesson 1

Consider the text:

This is some vacation, Tucker thought, rolling his eyes. He tugged his baseball hat tighter into his head. He hated when he got stuck helping his mom at work. Sitting around in a dusty museum looking at dishes was so boring. *I still don't understand why I can't just stay home alone,* he thought.

Steve Brezenoff, *Time Voyage*

Take a deeper look:

1. This passage is from a story about magically time traveling to the time of the *Titanic*. Tucker is one of the main characters in the story. Read the passage several times, paying attention to what Tucker thinks, what he does, and what the narrator says about him. What is Tucker's point of view about helping his mom at work? What evidence in the text helps you to know Tucker's point of view? Use the chart below to answer these questions.

Tucker's Point of View:	
Evidence (What Tucker thinks)	
Evidence (What Tucker does)	
Evidence (What the narrator says about Tucker)	

2. What is the tone of the passage? Which words, details, and images help you understand the tone of the passage?

Now you try it:

Write a paragraph about doing a chore you really do not like to do. Create a tone that is bitter and sarcastic. To create this tone, capture both your thoughts and your actions. Use the passage on the previous page as a model.

Tricky Tone

Student Lesson 1

Commentary and Suggestions for Teachers

Lesson Objective: to understand the relationship between point of view and tone and to create a tone that matches the point of view

Consider the text:

This passage is from the beginning of a story about Tucker and his friend Maya, who are spending their spring break helping Tucker's mother sort artifacts in a museum. As they sort through a box of artifacts, they find a magic ticket to travel back in time to the era of the *Titanic*. In this part of the story, Tucker has not yet experienced the magic of time travel. Have students read the passage several times, noting what Tucker thinks, what he does, and what the narrator says about him.

Take a deeper look:

1. Charts should look something like this:

Tucker's Point of View: Tucker thinks helping his mother at the museum during his spring break is boring. He would rather be home by himself.	
Evidence (What Tucker thinks)	"This is some vacation …" "I still don't understand why I can't just stay home alone …"
Evidence (What Tucker does)	He rolls his eyes He tugs his baseball hat tighter into his head
Evidence (What the narrator says about Tucker)	"He hated when he got stuck helping his mom at work." "Sitting around in a dusty museum looking at dishes was so boring."

The evidence from the text clearly establishes Tucker's point of view. It is important that students practice supporting ideas with text evidence rather than their own opinions.

2. The tone of the passage is bitter and reproachful. Of course, students do not have to use these exact words. They may call the tone "negative" or "grumbling" or use any similar words. Add students' appropriate tone words to the Tone Words Chart. Word choice that establishes the tone includes "hated," "stuck," "dusty," and "boring." All of these words indicate a negative attitude toward working in the museum. Details that establish the tone include the sarcasm of Tucker's first thought ("This is some va-

cation"), the statement that he hated getting stuck helping his mom, and referring to his work as the "dusty museum looking at dishes." Images include Tucker rolling his eyes and shoving his hat down on his head—both visual images of contempt.

Now you try it:

Paragraphs will vary, but students should establish a clear tone by capturing their thoughts and actions. Have students read their paragraphs to a partner and see if the partner can identify the tone. Students can then find a new partner and have that partner read the passage. (If the writer reads the passage, the listener will hear how the tone is supposed to sound, which will probably give it away.) By finding a new partner, the writer becomes the listener and can check to see if someone else understands the point of view and tone.

Tricky Tone

Student Lesson 2

Consider the text:

The *Titanic* stretched almost 900 feet long. Its rudder alone was bigger than Tucker's house. The huge hull was painted a shining black, and it seemed to stretch on forever in both directions. Tucker remembered a plaque he'd seen back at the museum: The *Titanic* was as long as three football fields and as tall as an eleven-story building.

A deep yellow stripe wrapped around the top of the ship, separating the black hull from the white at the top. Four tall smokestacks rose up from the deck like giant pillars. Against the bluegreen water of the harbor, *Titanic* was strikingly huge.

Steve Brezenoff, Time Voyage

Take a deeper look:

1. What is the purpose of this passage?

2. What is the tone of the passage? How does the purpose shape the tone?

Now you try it:

Describe something very large in or near your school. It could be a building, a tree, a sign, or some playground or sports equipment—anything that is huge. Your purpose is to help your readers clearly see what you are describing. Try to create an informative and serious tone. Use lots of detail and choose your words carefully.

Tricky Tone

Student Lesson 2

Commentary and Suggestions for Teachers

<u>**Lesson Objective:**</u> to understand the relationship between purpose and tone and to write to inform with a serious tone

Consider the text:

This passage comes from later in the story when Tucker and Maya have traveled back in time. Here they are looking at the actual *Titanic*. Students should read this passage with a partner several times and try to identify the purpose and tone.

Take a deeper look:

1. The purpose of this passage in broad terms is to inform or explain (often a choice on standardized tests). Students could also say that the purpose is to describe. The author uses word choice, detail, imagery, and figurative language ["it seemed to stretch on forever" (hyperbole); "smokestacks like giant pillars" (simile)] to give the reader an exact description of the size and scope of the *Titanic*.

2. The tone is serious and detached. The only judgment here is that the Titanic was huge, an objective judgment. There is no implication that it was dangerous or extravagant. The tone is determined by the purpose. The purpose is to give information, to describe; and the tone aligns with this purpose, remaining serious and objective. It is important to note here that a long work, such as a story, a novel, a chapter, or an article does not have to have the same tone throughout. The tone of the text in Lesson 1 from the same story is quite different from the tone in this passage. In Lesson 1, the purpose is to give insight into Tucker's dissatisfaction with helping his mother over spring break. The tone is negative, critical, and sarcastic. Here the purpose is to inform or describe. The tone is serious and objective. Purpose determines tone.

Now you try it:

Give students some time to plan and prewrite. They can list, cluster, brainstorm, or discuss ideas with a partner. It is important that they have time to plan before they write. You may even want to lead students through writing a model paragraph before they begin to work on their own. When they are finished with their writing, have them share their work with a group or the entire class. You may also want to post some student work around the classroom.

Tricky Tone

Student Lesson 3

Consider the text:

Magnets show people where to go. A compass needle always points north.
Earth's magnetic energy pulls it that way. Magnets help doctors see where
you are hurt. An MRI machine's powerful magnet helps make a picture of
the inside of your body. Magnets hold up pictures on a refrigerator. Credit
cards use magnets to pay for what you buy. Magnets are at work everywhere
you look!

Barbara Alpert, A Look at Magnets

Take a deeper look:

1. Who is the audience in this passage? What is the purpose?

2. What is the tone? What effects do audience and purpose have on tone?

Now you try it:

Write a sentence to finish the paragraph below. Your sentence should state the
main idea of the paragraph and show an enthusiastic tone toward the subject. Your
audience is other students your age.

**Playing sports is good for your health. Running makes your bones strong and
builds endurance. Sports help with coordination. If you learn gymnastics or
basketball, you have to learn muscle control and skill. Sports also help you
get along with people. Team sports like baseball, football, and volleyball teach
cooperation and respect for others. _____!**

Tricky Tone

Student Lesson 3

Commentary and Suggestions for Teachers

<u>Lesson Objective:</u> to understand the relationship between audience and tone and to craft an appropriate tone for the intended audience

Consider the text:

This passage is from an informational book about magnets. It is written for upper elementary students to explain the nature and use of magnets. Have students read the passage several times. You may have to explain that an MRI is a medical technique that uses magnets to see inside the body. It is interesting to note that the topic sentence of the paragraph is the last sentence. The other sentences are details that support the topic sentence. Students need to understand that topic sentences are not always the first sentence in a paragraph.

Take a deeper look:

1. The audience in this passage is students in the upper elementary grades. We know this since the passage is not highly technical; nor is it oversimplified. Vocabulary is straightforward and the concepts are at the introductory level. Sentences are short and examples are from everyday life. The purpose is to inform or explain.

2. The tone is both informative and enthusiastic. Most of the paragraph explains what magnets are used for—in clear, neutral language. The last sentence, however, expresses enthusiasm for magnets. It uses hyperbole, saying that magnets are at work everywhere; and it ends with an exclamation point, a sign of enthusiasm or excitement in writing.

Now you try it:

Students' sentences should express the main idea and show enthusiasm, much like the last sentence in Alpert's paragraph does. Students should write a sentence that looks something like this:

Sports help us in every way!

To extend this lesson, it would be helpful to have students examine their earlier writing to be certain the tone matches the audience and to check each paragraph for clear statements of main ideas.

Tricky Tone

Student Lesson 4

Consider the text:

> There was an Old Man with a beard,
>
> Who said, "It is just as I feared!—
>
> Two Owls and a Hen,
>
> Four Larks and a Wren,
>
> Have all built their nests in my beard."
>
> Edward Lear, *A Book of Nonsense*

Take a deeper look:

1. What is the purpose of this poem? How do you know?

2. Would you call the word choice in this poem formal or informal? How does the purpose affect the word choice?

Now you try it:

Complete the last two lines of the poem below. Your purpose is to entertain, and the language should be informal. Use Lear's poem above as a model.

There once was a silly, young dog
That wanted to write a short blog.
He sat and he planned,

_____

_____ .

Tricky Tone

Student Lesson 4

Commentary and Suggestions for Teachers

<u>**Lesson Objective:**</u> to understand the effect of purpose on word choice and tone and to write a poem that entertains

Consider the text:

This poem is a limerick, a short, funny (often silly), five-line poem. The rhyme scheme is aabba, and the poem has a regular rhythm. Some unexpected words ("Old Man," "Owls," "Hen," "Larks," "Wren") are capitalized in the poem, following the conventions of the time in which the poem was written. The capitalization does not have any particular importance to the meaning. This poem, like all poems, is best appreciated when read aloud. Read it first, modeling the rhythm and fun of it, and then have students read it aloud. It's easy and fun to get a limerick in your head and hear the rhythm all day long!

Take a deeper look:

1. The purpose of the poem is to amuse or entertain. We know the purpose because of the humor of the subject: an old man with eight birds' nests in his beard! Of course this is not possible or logical. The poem is a wild exaggeration of the size of the man's beard, and it creates a funny picture of a beard full of birds' nests.

2. The word choice is informal, conversational. The vocabulary is simple, without any academic language or words with multiple meanings. Word choice is determined by the purpose. The purpose is to entertain or amuse, so the poet chooses words that are light and easy to understand and contribute to the funny picture the poem creates.

Now you try it:

Let students have fun with this. It doesn't matter if the rhythm and rhyme is exactly right. The most important part of this activity is for students to understand purpose, levels of language formality, and how the two are connected. If they struggle with this activity, let them work in pairs or groups. Here is one way to complete the poem:

There once was a silly, young dog
That wanted to write a short blog.
He sat and he planned,
But he hadn't a hand,
So his plans stayed outside in the fog.

Tricky Tone

Student Lesson 5

Consider the text:

Microscopes are one of a forensic investigator's main tools. Almost everything that is brought back to a forensic lab is examined, a tiny piece at a time, using a microscope. The lenses in a microscope allow forensic experts to find tiny pieces of evidence that are invisible to the naked eye. They might see minute strands of fabric from the culprit's clothes. If the suspect has carried explosives, tiny particles may have become caught in the fabric. Forensic scientists can see them with a microscope.

Ross Piper, *Fingerprint Wizards: The Secrets of Forensic Science*

Take a deeper look:

1. What is the purpose of this passage? Is the audience a group of students or forensic scientists? How do you know?

2. What is the author's point of view? How does the author's point of view help create the tone?

Now you try it:

Write a paragraph with the following guidelines:

Subject: homework

Audience: your teacher

Purpose: to inform and convince

Point of view: you choose!

Tone: whatever matches your point of view

Share your paragraph with a partner or the class.

Tricky Tone

Student Lesson 5

Commentary and Suggestions for Teachers

Lesson Objective: to write with a tone that matches the purpose and point of view

Consider the text:

This passage is from a book that explains forensic science, the science used to establish evidence and facts in criminal investigations. This paragraph focuses on the microscope as one of the main tools used in forensic science. This is a good time to introduce the importance of point of view and its connection to tone. Although this passage is mainly informative, it does have a strong point of view: that microscopes are essential tools for forensic scientists. Students may need some vocabulary support: "naked eye" (vision with no assistance like a magnifying glass or a microscope), "minute" (tiny), "strands" (threads), "culprit" (criminal), "fabric" (cloth).

Take a deeper look:

1. The main purpose of the passage is to inform. The passage gives information about the use of microscopes in forensic science. But an underlying purpose is to convince readers of the importance of the microscope in forensic science. The audience is students. This is an introduction, not a scientific essay. There is virtually no scientific vocabulary, and details are drawn from common experience. Further, forensic scientists would already know this information.

2. The author's point of view is that microscopes are essential tools for the forensic investigator. All of the details in the paragraph support this point of view: Microscopes allow the scientists to see "tiny pieces of evidence," "minute strands of fabric," and "tiny particles [from explosives]." The author's point of view helps create tone by giving the passage a focus. The tone here is serious and informative, but it is also confident and forceful. The point of view is stated in the first sentence, and the details and tone give authority to that point of view.

Now you try it:

Students can choose to focus on the positive or negative side of homework. In other words, they decide their own point of view. However, they must write a well-supported paragraph with a clear purpose: to inform and convince. They will have to use lots of detail—facts, observations, examples—to support their point of view. Further, the tone should match the point of view. If, for example, the point of view is that homework has a detrimental effect on student health, the tone will probably be critical and judgmental. On the other hand, if the point of view is that homework is an important tool for learning, the tone will be more sympathetic and complementary. Give students time to gather their ideas and organize their thoughts before they write.

Tricky Tone

Student Lesson 6

Consider the text:

The soldiers were so amazed that they told Mulan's tale far and wide. The story of how a young girl became a warrior spread from person to person. It crossed mountains and oceans to many different countries. In Mulan's homeland people still sing about her.

It is hard to believe
that it could be so,
but now we have learned,
now we know
not to judge people
by how they look.
You, too, can be a hero
and have your tale told
or put in a book.

Michaela Morgan, Mulan

Take a deeper look:

1. This passage is from a story about a girl, Mulan, who disguises herself as a boy and becomes a skilled and famous leader and warrior. As a warrior, Mulan saves her family and helps her country. In this part of the book, Mulan reveals her true identity to the soldiers she has served with. What is the point of view of the soldiers in this passage? How do you know?

2. What is the tone of this passage? What evidence from the text supports what you identify as the tone of the passage?

Now you try it:

Read the first four sentences of the passage again. Now rewrite the sentences, keeping the basic situation but changing the tone. This time make the tone harsh, negative, and critical. Share your sentences with a partner.

Tricky Tone

Student Lesson 6

Commentary and Suggestions for Teachers

Lesson Objective: to identify and use the elements of voice that create tone

Consider the text:

Mulan is the story of a girl who disguises herself as a boy and becomes a soldier and great leader through her intelligence and leadership abilities. This passage is from the end of the story when Mulan reveals that she is a girl. Have students read the passage several times and think about point of view and tone.

Take a deeper look:

1. The soldiers admire and respect Mulan. They are amazed that she turns out to be a girl, but they celebrate her accomplishments and tell her story. The soldiers' point of view is revealed through word choice and detail. They are "amazed." They tell her story "far and wide." There is nothing in the diction or detail that indicates disapproval or anger. Their point of view about Mulan is celebratory and approving.

2. The tone of the passage, like the soldiers' point of view, is positive, approving, and admiring. The admiration goes even farther than the soldiers' point of view. This is strongly supported by evidence from the text: The story spreads "from person to person." It crosses "mountains and oceans to many different countries." People in her homeland "still sing about her." And everyone who hears her story learns "not to judge people by how they look."

Now you try it:

Students should see how meaning changes as an author changes the tone. Here is an example of how these sentences might be changed:

The soldiers were so disgusted and furious that they spread Mulan's deception far and wide. The story of how a young girl lied and pretended to be a boy spread from person to person. It spread like poison across mountains and oceans to many different countries. In Mulan's homeland people still curse her.

Tricky Tone

Student Lesson 7

Consider the text:

President Van Buren sent 7,000 soldiers to round up the Cherokee in May 1838. Entire families were arrested. They were ordered from their homes at bayonet point. They were supposed to receive food and supplies from the government, but most did not. Many were not even allowed to gather their belongings and needed supplies. They left home with only the clothes they were wearing.

As the Cherokee were dragged away, some white settlers tried to stop the soldiers from mistreating them. Others stole from the now-empty homes, while their former owners looked on.

Heather E. Schwartz, *Forced Removal: Causes and Effects of the Trail of Tears*

Take a deeper look:

1. This passage is from a book that describes the forced removal of more than 16,000 Cherokee from their homes in the southeastern United States to Indian Territory in present-day Oklahoma. The forced march of the Cherokee is called the Trail of Tears. What is the tone of this passage?

2. Complete the following chart with evidence from the passage that establishes the tone.

Tone:		
Evidence		
Word Choice	Detail	Imagery

Now you try it:

Talk to a partner about something you think is unfair or wrong. It could be the way someone is treated at school or something that is happening in your community. Explain what you think is unfair or wrong to your partner in a serious but critical way. Your partner should make a list of words, details, and images that you use to explain your position. Examine the list to be sure that your words, details, and images match your tone. Now trade places with your partner and go through the same procedures.

Tricky Tone

Student Lesson 7

Commentary and Suggestions for Teachers

Lesson Objective: to identify and use the elements of voice that create tone

Consider the text:

This passage is from a book about the causes and effects of the Trail of Tears, the forced removal of the Cherokee in the early 19th century. Students may find this passage disturbing, understandably so, but it is a part of our history. Students should read the passage several times, paying particular attention to how the author establishes tone.

Take a deeper look:

1. The tone of this passage is serious and critical. Although the criticism is not directly stated, it is inherent in the choices the author makes with respect to words, details, and images, most of which are negative and critical.

2. Charts should look something like this:

Tone: serious and critical		
Evidence		
Word Choice	Detail	Imagery
"round up" "were supposed to" "dragged away" "now-empty homes"	"Entire families were arrested." "They were supposed to receive food and supplies from the government, but most did not." "Many were not even allowed to gather their belongings and needed supplies." "… some white settlers tried to stop the soldiers from mistreating them." "Others stole from the now-empty homes …"	"They were ordered from their homes at bayonet point." "… the Cherokee were dragged away …" "… their former owners looked on."

Now you try it:

Students work with a partner for this activity. They should first talk about what they think is unfair or wrong. Then partner one explains what is unfair or wrong in a serious but critical tone, without anger or outbursts. Partner two writes down words, details, and images that explain what is wrong and why. Together they examine the list to be certain the words, details, and images match the tone. Then partner one and partner two change places and go through the same procedures.

Tricky Tone

Student Lesson 8

Consider the text:

This man had saved his life, which was something; but, further, he was the ideal master. Other men saw to the welfare of their dogs from a sense of duty and business expediency; he saw to the welfare of his as if they were his own children, because he could not help it …. He had a way of taking Buck's head roughly between his hands, and resting his own head upon Buck's, of shaking him back and forth, the while calling him ill names that to Buck were love names. Buck knew no greater joy than that rough embrace and the sound of murmured oaths, and at each jerk back and forth it seemed that his heart would be shaken out of his body so great was its ecstasy.

Jack London, *The Call of the Wild*

Take a deeper look:

1. This passage is from the novel *The Call of the Wild*. The main character and narrator is Buck, a dog that is taken to northwestern Canada to serve as a sled dog. The novel tells of Buck's good times and bad times as he learns to adapt to his surroundings. What is Buck's attitude toward the man who is described in this passage?

2. What is the tone of the passage? How does Buck's attitude affect the tone?

Now you try it:

Write a paragraph about something or someone you really love. It could be a place, a pet, a person, or even a game or some kind of food. Your tone should be joyful and admiring. Fill your paragraph with carefully chosen words, specific detail, and vivid images. Share your paragraph with a friend.

Tricky Tone

Student Lesson 8

Commentary and Suggestions for Teachers

Lesson Objective: to understand that attitude determines tone and to use words, details, imagery, and figurative language to shape the tone of writing

Consider the text:

The Call of the Wild is an adventure story. The main character, Buck, is a strong, intelligent dog that is taken from his home and sent to northwestern Canada to serve as a sled dog during the Klondike gold rush. He goes through some hard times and some good times, but eventually he reverts to the wild and joins a wolf pack. This passage describes one of the good times, Buck's relationship with a master who loves and cares for him. Students may need some support with vocabulary: "ideal" (best), "welfare" (health and safety), "ill names" (bad names, here said with love), "oath" (curse), and "ecstasy" (great happiness). As students read the passage, be sure they understand that Buck's master is saying bad words but saying them kindly. The dog understands the tone of voice, not the meaning of the words.

Take a deeper look:

1. Buck's attitude toward the man in this passage is one of absolute adoration. The man saved Buck's life and treats Buck like his own child. In return, Buck is totally devoted to his master. This attitude is made clear by the description of the man's embrace and his affectionate and gently teasing name-calling.

2. The tone of the passage is joyful and loving. Even the curses are affectionate. Since the story is told from Buck's point of view, his attitude determines the tone. Although the passage reveals the man's actions, we do not know his thoughts. We do, however, know Buck's thoughts ("he was the ideal master," "he saw to the welfare of his [dogs] as if they were his own children," "to Buck [the ill names] were love names," "Buck knew no greater joy than that rough embrace and the sound of murmured oaths," "it seemed that his heart would be shaken out of his body so great was its ecstasy"). Buck's thoughts are joyful and loving, which sets the tone of the passage.

Now you try it:

Give students some time to plan and prewrite before they write their paragraphs. Of course, sharing should be optional since some of their paragraphs may be very personal and students may not want to share them. Paragraphs could be funny too if, for example, they have chosen to write about their love of pizza. What is most important here is the focus on tone and attitude. Help students to understand that the attitude they have about their subject will determine the tone of their paragraph. And they shape tone with words, details, imagery, and figurative language.

Tricky Tone

Student Lesson 9

Consider the text:

We the People of the United States, in Order to form a more perfect Union, establish Justice, ensure domestic Tranquility, provide for the common defence, promote the general Welfare, and secure the Blessings of Liberty to ourselves and our Posterity, do ordain and establish this Constitution for the United States of America.

Preamble, The United States Constitution

Take a deeper look:

1. This is the introduction to the United States Constitution, the highest law of our country. It is called the Preamble to the Constitution, and it is a very important document. What is the purpose of the Preamble? Think about this carefully. It is not enough to say that the purpose is to introduce the Constitution!

2. What is the tone of the Preamble to the Constitution?

Now you try it:

Write a preamble to the code of conduct of your school. To help you with this difficult task, use the following sentence frame.

We the students and teachers of _____**, in order form a** _____**school, establish** _____**, ensure** _____**, and provide for the common** _____**, do establish this code of conduct for** _____.

Tricky Tone

Student Lesson 9

Commentary and Suggestions for Teachers

Lesson Objective: to demonstrate understanding of the connection between purpose and tone

Consider the text:

This is, of course, a difficult sentence for young people to understand. But it is important enough to be worth the effort. First, students may want to know why so many words are capitalized. This was a popular stylistic device used for emphasis in the 18th century. It has very little effect on meaning. Students also wonder about the spelling of "defense." Spelling it with a "c" instead of an "s" is just the way it was spelled back then. Rules of spelling, grammar, and punctuation change over time. Students may also need some vocabulary support: "ensure" (guarantee), "posterity" (future generations), "ordain" (order), and "establish" (create).

It is essential to read the Preamble with your students, to guide them through it. There are some aspects of the Preamble that students may not understand but are vital to comprehension: The framers of the Constitution included **all** citizens in the Preamble by saying "We the people of the United States" instead of "We the writers of this Constitution." That is a significant statement of their commitment to democratic ideals. They also call our government a "more perfect union," not a "perfect union." They understood that the Constitution will always be a flexible document, aiming for perfection but never achieving it. Finally, it is important to point out all of the strong verbs in the Preamble ("establish," "ensure," "provide for," "promote," "secure," "ordain," and "establish"). The verbs are active and precise, framing the goals of the government.

Take a deeper look:

1. The purpose of the Preamble is to explain why the Constitution was written and to set goals for the new government. Student answers may vary, but they should be able to understand these ideas and put them into their own words.

2. The tone is serious and forceful. The use of strong verbs and the specific nouns that go with the verbs support this tone. There is nothing ambivalent or confused in this statement. It is a clear, purposeful, and strong statement of goals and intent.

Now you try it:

Students' sentences should look something like this:

We the students and teachers of <u>Ourtown Elementary</u>, in order form a <u>more outstanding</u> school, establish <u>fair rules</u>, ensure <u>student safety</u>, and provide for the common <u>success</u>, do establish this code of conduct for <u>the entire Ourtown community</u>.

Tricky Tone

Student Lesson 10

Consider the text:

Once there was an elephant,

Who tried to use the telephant—

No! No! I mean an elephone

Who tried to use the telephone—

(Dear me! I am not certain quite

That even now I've got it right.)

Howe'er it was, he got his trunk

Entangled in the telephunk;

The more he tried to get it free,

The louder buzzed the telephee—

(I fear I better drop the song

Of elephop and telephong!)

Laura Elizabeth Richards, "Eletelephony"

Take a deeper look:

1. You simply have to read this poem aloud—several times—to get the full effect! See how fast you can read it! What is the purpose of the poem?

2. What is the tone? What elements of the poem create the tone?

Now you try it:

Complete the four-line poem below with words of your own choice. Try to create a tone similar to "Eletelephony." Have fun making up crazy words! If you want to make the poem longer, have fun with that, too.

Once there was a(n) _____ ,

Who tried to go to _____ —

No! No! I mean a(n) _____

Who tried to go to _____ .

Tricky Tone

Student Lesson 10

Commentary and Suggestions for Teachers

Lesson Objective: to demonstrate understanding of the connection between purpose and tone

Consider the text:

Students have to envision an old-style telephone with a cord. It may be that they have never even seen one! Just in case, it would be a good idea to show them a picture of a phone like the one here:

First, have students read the poem to themselves a few times just to get a feeling for the humor. Then have them read it aloud several times. It would be fun to have a timed contest to see which student can read the poem the fastest.

Take a deeper look:

1. The purpose of the poem is to entertain and amuse. On a deeper level, the purpose is to teach sounds and rhyme, which it does with humor and wit.

2. The tone is humorous and lighthearted. The author creates the tone through the use of rhyming nonsense words and the repetition of the way sounds are confused. The image of an elephant entangled in a telephone (both sight and sound) also contributes to the tone. In addition, there are lots of exclamation points in the poem. An exclamation point is an informal punctuation mark, rarely used in formal language. The exclamation points in this poem create a conversational tone, build the confusion, and help the reader understand and recreate the enthusiastic confusion of the narrator.

Now you try it:

Students' poems should look something like the one below. It doesn't matter if the rhythm and rhyme aren't perfect. Students should have fun with this activity and write lines that are humorous and lighthearted in tone. If students have trouble with rhymes, there are several good rhyming dictionaries online.

You might want to guide students through the writing process as a class before you set them loose on their own. First, students need to decide the words they want at the end of the first and fourth lines. These words should be at least two syllables long and should **not** rhyme. Then you combine the words into nonsense words to complete lines two and three. If students want to use different words than those provided in the poem frame, that is fine. Here is an example of what the poem might look like:

Once there was a <u>kangaroo</u>,
Who tried to go to <u>Michiroo</u>—
No! No! I mean a <u>kangagan</u>
Who tried to go to <u>Michigan</u>.

Tricky Tone

Student Lesson 11

Consider the text:

One of Sherlock Holmes's defects—if, indeed, one may call it a defect—was that he was exceedingly loath to communicate his full plans to any other person until the instant of their fulfilment. Partly it came no doubt from his own masterful nature, which loved to dominate and surprise those who were around him. Partly also from his professional caution, which urged him never to take any chances. The result, however, was very trying for those who were acting as his agents and assistants. I had often suffered under it, but never more so than during that long drive in the darkness. The great ordeal was in front of us; at last we were about to make our final effort, and yet Holmes had said nothing, and I could only surmise what his course of action would be.

Sir Arthur Conan Doyle, *The Hound of the Baskervilles*

Take a deeper look:

1. Sherlock Holmes is undoubtedly the most famous fictional detective of all times. What is the purpose of this passage?

2. The Sherlock Holmes stories have two main characters: Sherlock Holmes himself and his friend and assistant, Dr. John Watson. Here, as in most of the stories, Dr. Watson is the narrator, the one who tells the story. What attitude do Dr. Watson's words express toward Sherlock Holmes in this passage? List quotations from the passage that support what you identify as Dr. Watson's attitude toward Holmes.

Now you try it:

Think about a person or pet you like and respect. Now think about a trait of this person or pet's personality that makes life a little hard for you. Write a paragraph that describes this. Begin your paragraph like this:

One of _____'s defects—if, indeed, one may call it a defect—was that

_____

_____

_____

_____

_____

_____

Tricky Tone

Student Lesson 11

Commentary and Suggestions for Teachers

Lesson Objective: to examine how attitude and purpose shape tone and to create a tone that aligns with attitude and purpose

Consider the text:

This passage, from one of Arthur Conan Doyle's most famous stories about Sherlock Holmes, tells the story of how Holmes solves an attempted murder. The suspected murderer appears to be a legendary, supernatural, terrifying hound. However, the real murderer is an unscrupulous relative of the rightful heir to an estate in England. Holmes, of course, prevents the murder and solves the crime. Students may need some vocabulary support with this passage: "defect" (fault or flaw), "loath" (unwilling), "dominate" (rule or control), "trying" (difficult), "ordeal" (test), "surmise" (guess). The spelling of "fulfillment" is an older spelling of the word. If students have never read a Sherlock Holmes story, this would be an excellent enrichment activity. Doyle's stories are widely available online.

Take a deeper look:

1. The purpose of this passage is to give insight into Holmes's character and the relationship between Holmes and Watson. Holmes dominates Watson, but they do work well together. Watson admires Holmes but sometimes finds it difficult to cope with Holmes's unwillingness to share his plans for solving a murder.

2. Dr. Watson's attitude toward Sherlock Holmes is one of admiration and impatience. He admires Holmes's skill as a detective and is impatient with Holmes's unwillingness to share his plans. Watson's impatience, however, is tempered by his respect and appreciation for Holmes's masterful skill at detection. Here are the quotes that support this attitude:

Quote	Attitude it shows
"One of Sherlock Holmes's defects—if, indeed, one may call it a defect"	Watson finds Holmes's secrecy a fault but softens it by implying it may not be a fault at all.
"he was exceedingly loath to communicate his full plans to any other person until the instant of their fulfilment"	Holmes does not trust anyone with his plans until the mystery is solved.
"his own masterful nature, which loved to dominate and surprise those who were around him"	Watson respects Holmes's brilliance but finds him bossy and secretive.
"his professional caution, which urged him never to take any chances"	Watson acknowledges Holmes's extreme care with details.

Quote	Attitude it shows
"The result, however, was very trying for those who were acting as his agents and assistants"	Watson finds Holmes's caution and secrecy difficult to cope with.
"Holmes had said nothing, and I could only surmise what his course of action would be"	Holmes does not even trust Watson, his closest friend, and leaves him guessing as to how the crime will be solved.

Now you try it:

Give students some prewriting time and let them talk about the topic before writing. Paragraphs should express both what they admire and find difficult. When students are done with their paragraphs, let them share their work with a partner or the class.

As an extension, have students identify the attitude of a character from their independent reading and how that attitude is revealed. This could be an activity or a center during a reading block. Students could use the chart below or a similar one to record their thoughts.

Title and author of the book:		
Character:	Attitude:	Quotation that establishes the attitude:

Tricky Tone

Student Lesson 12

Consider the text:

The heat rapidly increased, and once again I looked up, shuddering as with a fit of the ague. There had been a second change in the cell …. The room had been square. I saw that two of its iron angles were now acute—two, consequently, obtuse. The fearful difference quickly increased with a low rumbling or moaning sound …. Its centre, and of course, its greatest width, came just over the yawning gulf [of the pit]. I shrank back—but the closing walls pressed me resistlessly onward. At length for my seared and writhing body there was no longer an inch of foothold on the firm floor of the prison. I struggled no more, but the agony of my soul found vent in one loud, long, and final scream of despair. I felt that I tottered upon the brink—I averted my eyes—

There was a discordant hum of human voices! There was a loud blast as of many trumpets! There was a harsh grating as of a thousand thunders! The fiery walls rushed back! An outstretched arm caught my own as I fell, fainting, into the abyss. It was that of General Lasalle. The French army had entered Toledo.

Edgar Allan Poe, "The Pit and the Pendulum," *The Works of Edgar Allan Poe, Volume II*

Take a deeper look:

1. This passage has a shift in tone. What are the two tones in the passage, and when does the tone shift?

2. Fill in the chart on the next page with examples of word choice, detail, imagery, and figurative language from this passage that help the reader understand the tones. Work in groups for this activity.

Tones in the Passage:			
Word Choice	Detail	Imagery	Figurative Language

Now you try it:

Write two paragraphs about struggling with a very difficult math problem. Your first paragraph should be about how hard the problem is and how much you struggle. The second paragraph should capture your excitement and relief when you finally solve the problem. Use exact words, specific detail, vivid images, and at least one figure of speech to create the changing tone of your passage. Share your work with a partner or the class.

Tricky Tone

Student Lesson 12

Commentary and Suggestions for Teachers

Lesson Objective: to understand and create a specific tone through word choice, detail, imagery, and figurative language

Consider the text:

In this story, an imprisoned and tortured man first suffers and then is finally rescued. Poe is famous for creating tension and terror in his stories. This story is one of his most famous and certainly lives up to Poe's reputation as the master of suspense. As with other challenging text, students may need some vocabulary support: "ague" (fever), "acute" (an angle less than 90 degrees), "obtuse" (an angle greater than 90 degrees), "centre" (older spelling of center), "gulf" (hole), "resistlessly" (without struggling—Poe often made up words), "seared" (burned), "writhing" (wriggling), "vent" (escape), "averted my eyes" (looked down), "discordant" (harsh), "abyss" (hole). Students do not have to know every single word in order to understand the passage. Since the text is challenging, it would be best for you to read it aloud several times, using good expression and building up the tension of the passage. Students will understand what is going on without certain knowledge of each word. Students may also like to read or listen to the entire story.

Take a deeper look:

1. The tone of the first paragraph is fearful and frightening. The narrator is about to be pushed into a pit by the burning, moving walls of his prison. The tone shifts in the second paragraph. Here the tone is joyful: The narrator is rescued by the French army.

2. Divide students into groups, and assign each group one column of the chart. Then have groups examine the passage carefully and fill out their column of the chart. Groups can share their results as you develop a class chart. Charts should look something like this:

Tones in the Passage: fearful and frightening, then joyful			
Word Choice	Detail	Imagery	Figurative Language
"shuddering"	"heat rapidly increased"	"heat rapidly increased" (touch)	"shuddering as with a fit of the ague" (simile)
"moaning"	"The room had been square. I saw that two of its iron angles were now acute—two, consequently, obtuse."	"The room had been square. I saw that two of its iron angles were now acute—two, consequently, obtuse." (sight)	"a loud blast as of many trumpets" (simile)

Tones in the Passage: fearful and frightening, then joyful			
Word Choice	Detail	Imagery	Figurative Language
"yawning"	"the closing walls pressed me resistlessly onward"	"a low rumbling or moaning sound" (sound)	"harsh grating as of a thousand thunders" (simile)
"seared and writhing"	"there was no longer an inch of foothold on the firm floor of the prison"	"my seared and writhing body" (touch)	
"agony"	"I struggled no more"	"the agony of my soul found vent in one loud, long, and final scream of despair" (sound)	
"discordant hum"	"I averted my eyes"	"discordant hum of human voices" (sound)	
"fiery"	"An outstretched arm caught my own as I fell, fainting, into the abyss"	"An outstretched arm caught my own as I fell, fainting, into the abyss" (touch, sight)	"The fiery walls rushed back" (personification)

Note that there is always overlap among diction, detail, and imagery. You can't have good detail without good diction, and effective imagery depends on both diction and detail.

Now you try it:

Students' paragraphs will vary. Help them to understand how to write so that the tone shifts, and encourage them to include exact words, specific detail, vivid images, and at least one figure of speech in their passage. Have students exchange their passages with a partner and see if their partners can identify the shift in tone.

This is an exercise that could be used to enhance any current writing. After this lesson, it would be helpful to have students look back at their drafts of current writing and encourage them to create tone with exact words, detail, vivid images, and figurative language.

Additional Resources for Tricky Tone

Tone Words Chart

accepting	disrespectful	neutral	Additional Tone Words
admiring	doubtful	objective	
affectionate	enthusiastic	peaceful	
angry	fearful	playful	
anxious	forceful	questioning	
approving	frightening	reproachful	
bitter	harsh	respectful	
bristling	haughty	sad	
calm	humorous	sarcastic	
cold	impartial	serious	
comical	indifferent	sharp	
complementary	informative	silly	
confident	joyful	straightforward	
confused	judgmental	sympathetic	
contemptuous	lighthearted	thoughtful	
critical	loving	threatening	
detached	mistrustful	uncertain	
didactic	mocking	whimsical	
disdainful	mysterious		

Examples and Nonexamples

Below are samples of text students can examine to help them understand the importance of creating tone in their writing. All text has tone of some sort, so the task here is to determine which passage most clearly and strongly develops tone. These examples and nonexamples allow students to:

- experience how word choice, detail, imagery, and figurative language help the reader identify and the writer create tone;
- use evidence to explain why a particular example most clearly and strongly expresses tone; and
- look at their own writing and see what they need to do to deepen and strengthen the tone.

Have students read all three examples and then use the chart to rank the passages' use of the elements of voice to create tone, citing evidence for their rankings.

New School Supplies by N. Dean

> Ex. 1: My new backpack was full of new school supplies. I had a big notebook, paper, some pencils, and markers. I also had a new lunch box, which was pretty cool. It was a pain carrying all of those things, but I do like having new things.

> Ex. 2: Having new school supplies begins my year like a sunrise over the mountains. Nervousness about a new school year is calmed by the bright newness of a spotless notebook and the smooth smell of clean paper. I love unsharpened pencils decorated with swirls and twists of reds and purples. The pencils seem to promise me that I will shine in school this year. I had dreamed of a matching backpack and lunch box, but when I got to the store, another combination called my name: a bright blue backpack and an orange insulated lunch bag, complete with matching ice packs. This will make my year!

> Ex. 3: I got a notebook, some paper, pencils, and a lunch box. It's nice to have new things.

Example	Tone	Elements of Voice Used to Develop Tone	Why the Tone is Unclear/Clear or Weak/Strong
Ex. 1			
Ex. 2			
Ex. 3			

Going to the Dentist by N. Danaher

Ex. 1: Going to the dentist is a scary thing, especially when you have a cavity.

Ex. 2: My mom tells me to stop shaking my foot and biting my nails, but I can't. She's not the one waiting to be called into a torture chamber. Oh, why couldn't I have been a better brusher? Did I really need all those candy bars? Did I really need to chew bubble gum all day? And now here I am, eleven years old with my first cavity. What's taking so long? I've waited an eternity! Maybe they forgot about me. Maybe my cavity disappeared. Never mind. The hygienist just called my name. Oh, please don't hurt me! I'll brush two times, no, three times a day! I'll even floss! Someone please tell me this is a bad dream!

Ex. 3: Last week, I got a cavity filled. It hurt a lot. The worst part was when I heard the drill.

Example	Tone	Elements of Voice Used to Develop Tone	Why the Tone is Unclear/Clear or Weak/Strong
Ex. 1			
Ex. 2			
Ex. 3			

Student Work

When we first started this project, there was some concern that the texts, concepts, and activities were too hard for elementary students. Although we firmly believe in the importance of rigor and challenge, we did not want students to be overwhelmed or to lose the joy of reading and writing. It was therefore of utmost importance to field test selected lessons in each chapter.

We tested the lessons with two wonderful groups of students: third graders at P.K. Yonge Developmental Research School in Gainesville, Florida, and fifth graders at Our Lady of the Wayside School in Chicago, Illinois. The results were gratifying. Students found the lessons challenging but very engaging. Enthusiasm ran high, and students worked hard to understand the passages and complete the activities. In short, students loved the lessons!

Many students did need some support with the difficult language of some of the passages. But no one wanted to give up. For example, when Florida third graders worked on Lesson 3 from the Irresistible Imagery chapter, they needed some support in order to understand the effects of a blizzard (many of the students had never even seen snow). And they just didn't understand what the rope between the house and barn was for. The teacher showed them pictures of a farm in a blizzard and then read the passage several times again. By the third reading, faces began to light up. "Oh! I get it," echoed throughout the room. It was heartening. When we debriefed the lesson, students agreed that learning through reading is fun and writing is "the best."

We have included several examples of student work from each chapter. The student work isn't perfect, but it's real. It bears witness to students' understanding of the elements of voice and the importance of careful reading and crafted writing.

Wonderful Words

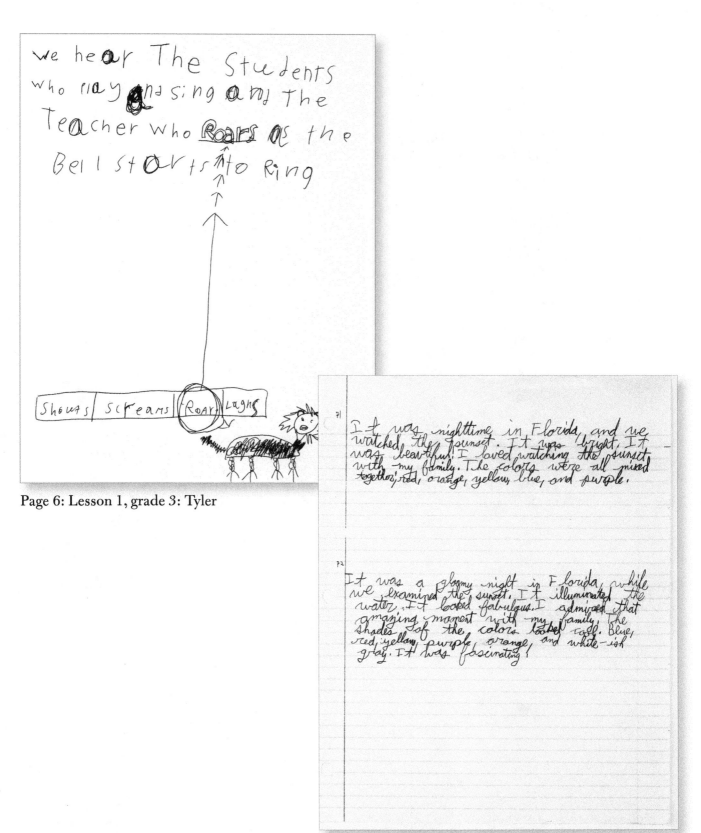

we hear The Students
who play gnasing and the
Teacher who Roars as the
Bell starts to Ring

| Shouts | Screams | Roar | Laghs |

Page 6: Lesson 1, grade 3: Tyler

It was nighttime in Florida, and we
watched the sunset. It was bright. It
was beautiful! I loved watching the sunset
with my family. The colors were all mixed
together; red, orange, yellow, blue, and purple.

It was a gloomy night in Florida, while
we examined the sunset. It illuminated the
water. It looked fabulous. I admired that
amazing moment with my family. The
shades of the colors looked cool. Blue,
red, yellow, purple, orange, and white-ish
gray. It was fascinating!

Page 22: Lesson 8, grade 5: Benjamin

Dazzling Detail

By Taylor

Planning:
My favorite color is Blue . It makes me feel
Save and brave and calms me down

Some things that are ~~purple~~ Blue are

the sky and waves at the beach

Poem or Paragraph:

Poem

When your sad don't feel bad just look for blue

in the sky. When your at the beach look around you
and all you will see is the colar blue it makes me
feel warm inside and when I'm sad I do not cry I
whipe the tears from my eye. So now you know how
when I see the colar blue I want to squweel.

Page 42: Lesson 2, grade 3: Taylor

Boom! The lights go out. I 'm alone.
I call my parents name. No answer.
I call them again. Still no answer.
In my head, I am completly
badazzled. Just me alone. The front
door is unlocked and wide open,
the windows are shattered! I
slowly walk down the stairs. The
last stair crecks as I walk. I
lock the door. A flash of black smoke
appers and a face appers,

Page 62: Lesson 10, grade 5: Kira

Irresistible Imagery

A HOT SUMMER DAY

On a hot day I like to eat popcicles and go to the pool I hear splash of people jumping in the pool I hear the BOING! of the diveing bord I taste the cloreen in the pool I taste the ice cold lemonaid I feel so Relaxed when I'm at the pool

By Taylor

Page 78: Lesson 3, grade 3: Taylor

The steak was miles high, hot and juicy, and completely irresistable. It smelled like heaven, no better, like something impossible to make. It tasted like victory, getting rich, and winning every single trophy by yourself.

Page 82: Lesson 5, grade 5: Benjamin

Fabulous Figurative Language

Lorenco

Her smile was like the smarfs.
He ran like a mustang.
The pencil was sharp as a broken piece of glass.

Page 113: Lesson 3, grade 3: Lorenzo

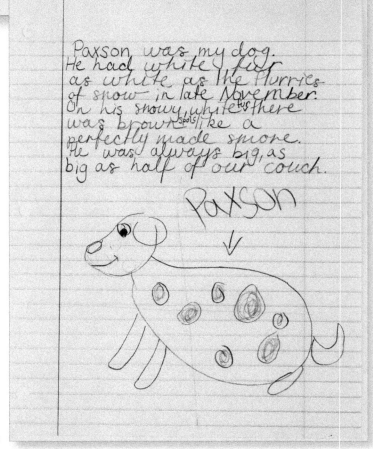

Paxson was my dog.
He had white fur
as white as the flurries
of snow in late November.
On his snowy white was there
was brown spots like a
perfectly made smore.
He was always big, as
big as half of our couch.

Paxson
↓

Page 115: Lesson 4, grade 5: Paige

Tricky Tone

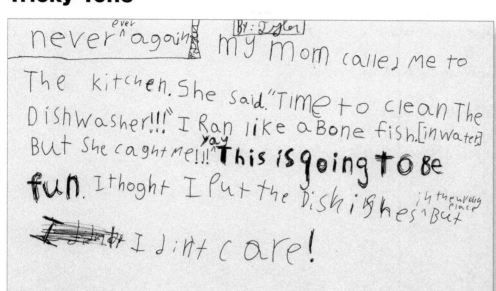

never ^ever ^again [By: Tyler] my mom (alled) me to The kitchen. She said. "Time to clean The Dishwasher!!!" I Ran like a Bone fish.[in water] But She caght me!!! ^yay This is going To Be fun. I thoght I put the Dish ishes ^in the wrong place ˌBut ~~I dont~~ I dint c are!

Page 145: Lesson 1, grade 3: Tyler

Homework is hard. I do not favor it. It uses all of our energy. Say that it has been a long day and you just want to take a nap but you cant because you have homework. Or you have been wanting to see this blockbuster film but you cant because you have home work. Homework ruins my day

Page 154: Lesson 5, grade 5: Paige

Sources for the Passages

Texts in the Public Domain

Burnett, Frances Hodgson, *The Secret Garden*

Doyle, Sir Arthur Conan, *The Hound of the Baskervilles*

Grahame, Kenneth, *The Wind in the Willows*

Irving, Washington, "The Legend of Sleepy Hollow"

Kipling, Rudyard, *The Jungle Book*

Lear, Edward, *A Book of Nonsense*

London, Jack, *The Call of the Wild*

London, Jack, *White Fang*

Longfellow, Henry W., "Hiawatha's Childhood"

Marshall, Logan, "The Cyclops," *Myths and Legends of All Nations*

Noyes, Alfred, "Pirates," *Collected Poems*

Poe, Edgar Allan, "The Pit and the Pendulum," *The Works of Edgar Allan Poe, Volume II*

Preamble, The United States Constitution

Richards, Laura Elizabeth, "Eletelephony"

Sewell, Anna, *Black Beauty*

Stevenson, Robert Louis, "The Wind"

Whipple, Wayne, *The Story of Young Abraham Lincoln*

Capstone/Heinemann Library Books

Allen, K. (2010). Disgusting History Series: *The Horrible, Miserable Middle Ages: The Disgusting Details about Life During Medieval Times*. North Mankato, MN: Capstone.

Alpert, B. (2012). Science Builders Series: *A Look at Magnets*. North Mankato, MN: Capstone.

Brezenoff, S. (2012). Return to Titanic Series: *Time Voyage*. North Mankato, MN: Capstone.

Burchett, J. and Vogler, S. (2012). Wild Rescue Series: *Rainforest Rescue*. North Mankato, MN: Capstone.

Burgan, M. (2015). What You Didn't Know About the American Revolution Series: *The Untold Story of the Black Regiment: Fighting in the Revolutionary War*. North Mankato, MN: Capstone.

Capek, M. (2015). The Civil War Series: *The Battle over Slavery: Causes and Effects of the U.S. Civil War*. North Mankato, MN: Capstone.

Dahl, M. (2013). Sports Illustrated Kids Bedtime Books: *Goodnight Baseball*. North Mankato, MN: Capstone.

Dell, P. (2011). Captured History Series: *Man on the Moon: How a Photograph Made Anything Seem Possible*. North Mankato, MN: Capstone.

Falkner, B. (2014). *Northwood*. North Mankato, MN: Capstone.

Fandel, J. (2014). Poet in You Series: "The First Snowfall" from *Thorns, Horns, and Crescent Moons: Reading and Writing Nature Poems* by Jennifer Fandel and Connie Colwell Miller. North Mankato, MN: Capstone.

Frisch-Schmoll, J. (2015). Ice Age Animals Series: *Ground Sloths*. North Mankato, MN: Capstone.

Giulieri, A. (2012). Engage Literacy Blue Series: *The Banana Spider*. North Mankato, MN: Capstone.

Higgins, M. (2015). Ice Age Animals Series: *Dodos*. North Mankato, MN: Capstone.

Lindeen, M. (2012). Wonder Readers Series: *Parks of the U.S.A*. North Mankato, MN: Capstone.

Lockwood, V. (2015). The Magnificent Lizzie Brown Series: *The Magnificent Lizzie Brown and the Devil's Hound*. North Mankato, MN: Capstone.

Martin, I. (2015). Animal Kingdom Questions and Answers Series: *Amphibians: A Question and Answer Book*. North Mankato, MN: Capstone.

Miller, C. C. (2014). Poet in You Series: "Visiting the Buffalo" from *Thorns, Horns, and Crescent Moons: Reading and Writing Nature Poems* by Jennifer Fandel and Connie Colwell Miller. North Mankato, MN: Capstone.

Morgan, M. (2014). Traditional Tales Series: *Mulan*. North Mankato, MN: Capstone.

Mortensen, L. (2015). We Shall Overcome Series: *Voices of the Civil Rights Movement: A Primary Source Exploration of the Struggle for Racial Equality*. North Mankato, MN: Capstone.

Otfinoski, S. (2015). You Choose: History Series: *The Story of Juneteenth: An Interactive History Adventure*. North Mankato, MN: Capstone.

Piper, R. (2008). Extreme! Series: *Fingerprint Wizards: The Secrets of Forensic Science*. North Mankato, MN: Capstone.

Poole, H. (2014). Fiction Picture Books Series: *Clara's Crazy Curls*. North Mankato, MN: Capstone.

Powling, C. (2014). Traditional Tales Series: *East of the Sun, West of the Moon*. North Mankato, MN: Capstone.

Radomski, K. (2015). The Revolutionary War Series: *Battle for a New Nation: Causes and Effects of the Revolutionary War*. North Mankato, MN: Capstone.

Rau, D. M. (2012). Sports Illustrated Kids. Sports Training Zone Series: *Sports Nutrition for Teen Athletes: Eat Right to Take Your Game to the Next Level*. North Mankato, MN: Capstone.

Salas, L. P. (2008). Poetry Series: "Sunshine," *Flashy, Clashy, and Oh-So Splashy: Poems about Color*. North Mankato, MN: Capstone.

Schaefer, L. M. (2008). Understanding Differences Series: *Some Kids Use Wheelchairs*. North Mankato, MN: Capstone.

Schwartz, H. E. (2015). Cause and Effect: American Indian History Series: *Forced Removal: Causes and Effects of the Trail of Tears*. North Mankato, MN: Capstone.

Schwartz, H. E. (2010). Disgusting History Series: *The Foul, Filthy American Frontier: The Disgusting Details About the Journey Out West*. North Mankato, MN: Capstone.

Shaffer, J. J. (2013). Monster Science Series: *Vampires and Light*. North Mankato, MN: Capstone.

Slade, S. (2014). The Science of Speed Series: *The Science of Bicycle Racing*. North Mankato, MN: Capstone.

Snedden, R. (2012). The Web of Life Series: *Adaptation and Survival*. Chicago, IL: Raintree Library.

Wegwerth, A. L. (2015). Smithsonian Little Explorer. Dinosaurs and Prehistoric Animals Series: *Tyrannosaurus Rex*. North Mankato, MN: Capstone.

Notes

Notes

Maupin House
capstone

At Maupin House by Capstone Professional, we continue to look for professional development resources that support grades K–8 classroom teachers in areas, such as these:

Literacy	Language Arts
Content-Area Literacy	Research-Based Practices
Assessment	Inquiry
Technology	Differentiation
Standards-Based Instruction	School Safety
Classroom Management	School Community

If you have an idea for a professional development resource, visit our Become an Author website at:
http://www.capstonepub.com/classroom/professional-development/become-an-author/

There are two ways to submit questions and proposals.

You may send them electronically to:
proposals@capstonepd.com

You may send them via postal mail. Please be sure to include a self-addressed stamped envelope for us to return materials.

Acquisitions Editor
Capstone Professional
1 N. LaSalle Street, Suite 1800
Chicago, IL 60602